# OLD MAN'S STORY

'You look after country...

Country he look after you.'

# OLD MAN'S STORY

The last thoughts of Kakadu Elder Bill Neidjie

Bill Neidjie as told to Mark Lang
Photographs by Mark Lang

Aboriginal
Studies Press

First published in 2015 by Aboriginal Studies Press

© Bill Neidjie and Mark Lang 2015

Reprinted 2020

All rights reserved. No part of this book may be reproduced or transmitted in any form or by any means, electronic or mechanical, including photocopying, recording or by any information storage and retrieval system, without prior permission in writing from the publisher. The Australian Copyright Act 1968 (the Act) allows a maximum of one chapter or 10 per cent of this book, whichever is the greater, to be photocopied by any educational institution for its education purposes provided that the educational institution (or body that administers it) has given a remuneration notice to Copyright Agency Limited (CAL) under the Act.

Aboriginal Studies Press is the publishing arm of the Australian Institute of Aboriginal and Torres Strait Islander Studies.

GPO Box 553, Canberra, ACT 2601

Phone: (61 2) 6246 1183
Fax:     (61 2) 6261 4288
Email:  asp@aiatsis.gov.au
Web:   www.aiatsis.gov.au/asp/about.html

National Library of Australia Cataloguing-in-Publication entry : (paperback)

Creator: Neidjie, Bill, 1913-2002, author.

Title: Old Man's story/Bill Neidjie; Mark Lang (author and photographer).

ISBN: 9781922059949 (paperback)
       9781922059956 (ebook:pdf)

Subjects: Aboriginal Australians — Australia — Anecdotes. Aboriginal Australians — Australia — Social life and customs.

Other Creators/Contributors: Lang, Mark, author, photographer.

Dewey Number: 305.89915

Front cover: Bill Neidjie. Back cover: Heart-shaped rock at Ubirr. Photographs by Mark Lang.

Aboriginal and Torres Strait Islander people are advised that this publication contains names and images of people who have passed away.

# FOREWORD

**A memory of *Old Man's Story* — Big Bill Neidjie — My great uncle**

Not only is this a rare opportunity, but it is an honour and an enormous privilege to write the foreword for a book of such significant spiritual history that still lives today.

I say thank you to Big Bill Neidjie, my great uncle, not only for your teachings over the decades but your passion and resilience in ensuring your stories are passed on to future generations. I honour you.

Every time I arrive back home in Bunitj Country, in Kakadu, I think and feel about the connection to country and how the land and its habitat identifies us with a complete sense of oneness, how it is all dedicated to maintaining an order, and a balance.

Old Man told me about where I'm from and what my inherited responsibilities would be. He reminded me that to be Aboriginal is to be the land and everything around it and on it. He used to say:

'My children got to hang onto this story. This important story, I hang onto this story all my life, my father tell me this story, my children can't lose it.'

I've always held onto those times with Old Man in a special place; close to my heart, close to my spirit. Whenever the thunder rolls and crashes, I'm reminded of his voice. Sitting there with him looking out over the Magela flood plains, this deep voice, filled with authority, would fit just in the right way with the scenes and the things he was describing.

I was reminded how we all have to return home one day to take up our responsibilities. I always feel this huge obligation but nonetheless I have a real sense of pride and it's one that I'm proud to maintain.

It would not be possible to continue the cultural practices and pass these stories on without Big Bill. He has enabled us to do that.

He taught me that our duties take many forms and is lived every day of our lives. He used to say it is important to teach the sacred knowledge to each new generation and that this learning is absorbed over a lifetime through the teachings and examples of the elders and in a series of ceremonies.

## FOREWORD

I felt like I belonged when he spoke to me. He told me about my place in the landscape, my place in country.

The sounds, the colours, the special stories of special places just flowed from him. He was both inspirational and at times intimidating by demanding authority about the 'humbug' world destroying our cultural inherited responsibilities.

But most of all he was gentle yet he sounded so powerful. He lived a proud and often very tough life. He possessed great presence and he walked tall — not for nothing was he known as 'Big Bill'.

'Look at your country, your people's country. You can see it and you can feel it.'

Throughout my career as an athlete, advocate and now as a Senator in the Australian Parliament, I've held those times close and used them as both a guide and strength to know what it is I am standing for as an Aboriginal woman in Parliament.

There are many great Australians, past and present that have shaped our views of Australia. But for me, the voice of Old Man remains the most insightful and dignified measure of what makes the land so vital. He understood what country means and how important it is to sustain our tradition.

Big Bill spoke for the Earth. Ma, Bor bor.

Senator Nova Peris OAM
July 2015

# CONTENTS

## THE FIRST STORY
1

## THE DRY SEASON
15

## THE WET SEASON
109

## BACK TO THE DRY
173

Jim Jim Falls, Kakadu.

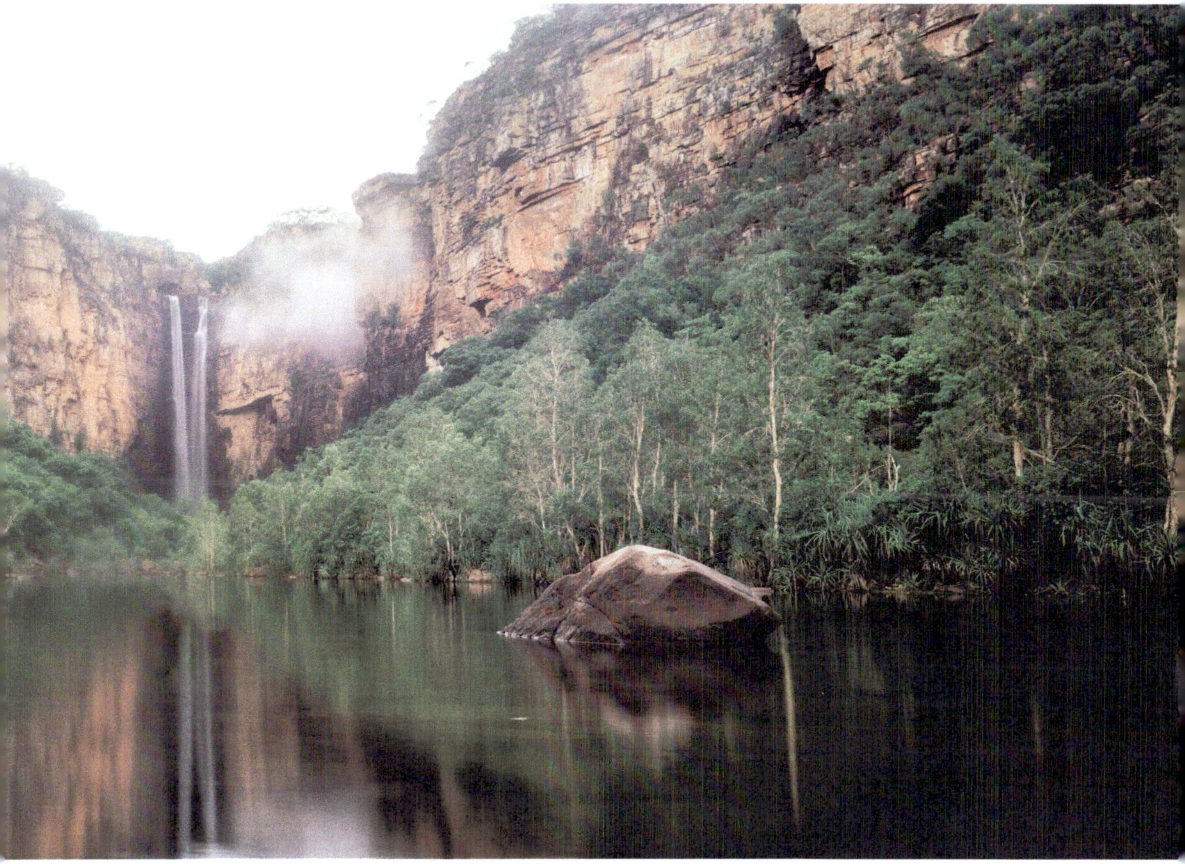

Wildhoney
lily,
geese

Big Bill's
Camp

Camp of
Dolly Yanmalu

Nabádi
High ground –
Spring with fresh
water

Nawarrkpil
Big Cave
for camping
in wet

Walkarr
Shelter
Bill's hand
stencil
as a
child

Lots of Yams

Maraul
Dry Season
Camp

KAKAD

Paperb

Map of the Old Man's country.
Produced by Jane Moore.

## PROLOGUE

One day, twenty years ago, I sold house and home so that I could travel Australia and photograph the landscape for a book, my own book, dedicated to this land that I love. It was something I had promised myself that I would do one day.

Two years later, I rolled into Kakadu.

Kakadu is a World Heritage-listed National Park in the Northern Territory of Australia, one of the largest and most diverse parks on the whole continent, and a place of exceptional beauty. I dwelt there for three weeks during the early Wet Season; a time of sudden afternoon storms, floods, and lightning in the night.

In the time that I spent in Kakadu I shot some reasonable pictures too, being fortunate enough on my first day to visit the Chief Ranger at Park Headquarters to obtain my photographic permit. He recommended that I head straight for Jim Jim Falls (one of the principal attractions of the Park), explaining that because of rising floodwaters the road to the falls was due to be closed the next day until the end of the Wet, another four months away. So it was a case of now or never.

I left straightaway, and found the falls shrouded in low cloud. They disappeared and re-emerged as gentle rain passed through the gorge, their sound echoing against the walls. I sat on a rock and watched them for hours until a rumble of thunder broke my trance. It was a sight of incredible beauty, and I had it all to myself; the last visitor for the year.

Days later the monsoon rains started in earnest. The floodwaters looked like they were rising fast and I might be flooded in there for months. Much of the Park was disappearing under water; there were few places that I could visit safely, so I bailed out of there and headed for drier country.

I was happy enough to leave Kakadu for I felt that I had some good pictures, but resolved that I would return there during a Dry Season when the country would be more accessible; I could dwell there longer and explore the place more thoroughly.

\*\*\*

# PROLOGUE

A year later, and despite having experienced some of the extremes of the country — from the howling snowbound wastes in the mountains of Tasmania to the utterly parched and scorching silence of the Simpson Desert — there was still so much more to see. However, I had reached a point where I felt that I had seen a lot of the country, and yet I still had not got to know the place. My relationship with this amazing land was rather like a passing friendship; just as the acquaintance was deepening it was time to go, to move on, back to the road again. In my heart, there was a growing awareness of the immense spirit of the land, and with that came a realisation that the country would not reveal its secrets to me easily. Perhaps I might learn more if I could just learn to be still and dwell awhile.

I had reached a stage where I was wanting to spend time with Aboriginal people, for they have an intimate link with the country that comes from having dwelt upon it for countless years, living with the knowledge that they are part of it, and it is part of them. I felt that any book devoted to the Australian landscape, as mine was, would need to have an Aboriginal perspective within it. I would only gain that understanding if I spent some time in the company of these people, ideally with a tribal elder who might teach me something about his country.

So, later in the year, I returned to Kakadu.

I had made friends with some of the Kakadu Rangers at East Alligator River during my previous visit. Principally Trevor Weir, who was not only a Ranger, but also an artist, with a friendly disposition and an eccentric sense of humour whose company I greatly enjoyed. Trevor had the contract to provide surveillance over the Aboriginal art sites at Ubirr. As a guardian of these ancient places he was answerable to one of the traditional owners of that country, Big Bill Neidjie, who had become a good friend and lived close to where Trevor was staying. Bill was happy for the visiting public to enjoy and learn about the art, just as long as there was someone like Trevor keeping an eye open for the occasional vandal who might damage these ancient rock paintings, which, as a traditional owner, were Bill's responsibility.

Bill was an old man these days, and he lived with his family in a house close behind the East Alligator Ranger Station from where he could be transported to hospital easily should there be a sudden crisis with his health, for he was fragile, confined to his wheelchair, and hardly able to leave his house.

PROLOGUE

I hoped that Bill might be able to help me find someone to 'learn me up' and school me in Aboriginal culture, so, with Trevor's help, I drafted a letter to Bill. If I saw him I would give it to him with a copy of one of my books, just to show him my work. I hoped we might have a chat to see if he could recommend anybody, and maybe give me some advice as to where to go, and who to see.

I had never met Bill before; only read about him. It seemed that everyone who had heard of him wanted to meet him, for he came with a formidable reputation as 'Big Bill' Neidjie, a huge man over six feet tall who commanded great respect. And he was very well-known, having had two books of his thoughts published already.

How would I go? I wondered.

What would he say?

\*\*\*

Days later I was sitting in my truck near East Alligator River outside the Border Store beside Cahill's Crossing, the gateway to Arnhem Land. It was lunchtime and I was enjoying a snack when a green utility wagon pulled up alongside, and the driver stepped out to enter the store.

Alone in the passenger seat was a big old Aboriginal man staring out of the windscreen looking at the tourists under the sunshades, especially the pretty girls. His huge head was crowned with white hair, and the lines on his face spoke of a deep and solemn presence. As I looked at him, he turned his head to look my way with strong dark eyes that seemed to look right through me.

There was no doubt in my mind who he was. This was Old Man Bill.

I stepped out of my truck, and with book and letter in hand walked round to the passenger window. Nervously, I introduced myself and gave him my book with trembling hands. He flicked through the pages and thanked me for it, tucking the letter away in a pocket to read later.

'You got cigarette?' was the first thing I heard him say, in a voice as deep as the river.

'Sorry Bill, I don't smoke,' was my feeble reply.

'Hmm, no matter. Well, I see you then.'

I shook his hand, warm, like soft leather, wished him well, and drove away.

\*\*\*

# PROLOGUE

I was camped with the Seasonal Rangers at the Training Camp, which was where Trevor lived, in a battered old Parks caravan. Trevor had two members of staff looking after the surveillance at Ubirr; Ian, who lived at Jabiru, and Jamie, a friendly mischievous-looking geezer who lived onsite in another caravan from where jazz could be heard playing through the night.

Nearby was a demountable house, and here were installed Kate and Darrin, both working for the Park during the Dry Season as Rangers, but both totally unsuited to sharing a house together.

One morning I was having a cuppa with Darrin in his house. He looked out of the window and said, 'You know, you should meet up with Jacob. He's an important man too.'

He was right — Ubirr was an art site where the responsibility for its upkeep lay with two tribal groups who shared the country together. These groups were headed by the two traditional owners, Big Bill and Jacob. There, outside in the morning light, sitting on a log in front of a fire with a huge black hat on his head was a fine-looking man hunched over a barbecue plate, frying fish.

Jacob.

I went over to say hello.

He was friendly, but enjoying the peace of the fire, he didn't seem to feel like talking.

I thought, however, that I should tell him what my intentions were while I was camped here, for this was his country too. I told him that I was writing a book and needed to spend time with Aboriginal people in order to learn something of their ways. He nodded and said nothing; for it's a request that white people make to Aboriginal folk all the time. However, he seemed interested in helping me, and told me we should catch up to talk about this some more. Maybe we'd work together, no promises.

He turned back to the fire, and the fish cooking there.

Weeks later, Jacob arranged a permit for me to come across the river into Arnhem Land and visit him in Oenpelli where he lived in a little tin house in the shade of a giant banyan tree. He said that he had a book about his life that he wanted to write, and that maybe I could help him and learn about Aboriginal culture along the way. After an hour we agreed that we would work together, and shook hands on the matter.

We never spoke to each other again.

PROLOGUE

\*\*\*

The days were passing while I waited for word from Jacob. Each time I tried to contact him there were messages of him being away on funeral business, or bogged down with community meetings, with no further news.

The country began to take on a parched look as the Dry Season bit, and the air was full of smoke from burning-off the speargrass. My reservoir of hope was drying up as well.

However, in that time Trevor had taken Jamie and me around to Bill's house near the Ranger Station to say hello. Old Man had sat in his wheelchair and watched us, saying little at first, but soon he opened up and began to ask me about my journey and made me feel welcome in his country.

After that I became a frequent visitor to Bill's house, Jamie too, for he enjoyed our company. On the weekends I would take Bill some fruit, fresh from Darwin. We would sit on the verandah and Bill would tell stories from his amazing past, but slowly and with great effort, for a lifetime of smoking had left his lungs shot to pieces and he would have to pause frequently to summon enough breath to finish a tale.

I secretly wished I could work with Bill instead of Jacob, for, more than any other elder, he had been prepared to share the wisdom of his people with the whitefella world; a caring knowledge based on living in harmony with the natural world over many thousands of years. This, I felt, was the learning that I needed, but I feared that Bill would be too weak for the task, being a fragile old man in his eighties. Besides, two books of his thoughts had been published already; why would he want to do more?

Who was he, this charismatic old man?

From what I could gather, he had been born sometime early in the century near the banks of the East Alligator River into the Bunitj clan of his father and was now one of the last of his tribe to speak the Gagudju language. Bill had grown up in this area, and lived here, at Ubirr, in the tribal lands that his people had inhabited for countless generations before him. He'd been brought up the traditional way with respect to the Gagudju Law by his father, grandfather and uncles, and his family had taught him how to hunt and fish, and how to read the rhythms and seasons of his country — how to 'look after country', as his people had done for so long.

# PROLOGUE

When Bill was maybe twelve years old his father died and his mother, Lucy, took him to live up near Cape Don on the Cobourg Peninsula. Here he stayed beside the sea for five years or so with his mother's family and an old buffalo hunter, Billy Manilungu, who schooled Bill in Gagudju Law; an absolute inflexible framework of belief that governed their everyday life. This was a rock solid system of values, for which Bill, as one of the last of the 'old people' still stood, amidst a modern world where the old values were changing.

He had worked all of his active life, returning to East Alligator to work with the buffalo hunters for a short while, and then to the mill at Mountnorris Bay for some years, eventually taking to the sea carting timber in a lugger and working the coast from the mill at Croker Island to Darwin. He would have been an impressive sight in those days, for people used to refer to him as 'Big Bill Neidjie', and early pictures show a muscular man of at least six foot three, with immense physical strength and great presence.

But his country was 'singing out for him', so he returned to the East Alligator area during the Second World War, living beside the sea at Paw Paw Beach, close by the mouth of the river. It was while he was there that he went through his initiation in an Ubarr ceremony; one of the most important events in a Gagudju man's life where the terrified initiates were surrounded by elders and threatened with spears if they didn't listen close.

Upon the death of his father, a traditional owner, the huge responsibility of looking after his country had passed to Bill.

Now, after the buffalo hunters, came the rest of the 'balanda' whitefella world, with an entirely different set of values based on money, wealth and property; values which were directly opposed to the harmonious lifestyle enjoyed by the tribal people, who, over the centuries, had lived with deep respect to their land.

However, it was during the sixties and seventies that the greatest threat to their country appeared. Substantial deposits of high-grade uranium ore had been discovered and, in spite of the protests from the tribal elders, leases for exploration and mining had already been granted. This was in the era before land rights, when Aboriginal people had little say in what happened to their country. Bill Neidjie's response in defence of his country took several forms.

Firstly, he was instrumental, with other tribal traditional owners in the area, in negotiating the terms that declared his tribal land as a National Park, thereby preventing the granting of any further uranium leases and also, importantly,

PROLOGUE

enabling the whitefella world to come to his country to learn about the values that lie within the traditional Aboriginal attitude to life and to land. Here the black man and the white man could work together and look after the country.

Furthermore, his own philosophy, based upon the values that had been handed down to him, were expressed in two books: *Kakadu Man*, and *Story About Feeling*, which have both moved countless people to realise that the traditional attitude to country was one of caring for the land, and of looking beyond tomorrow.

> 'You look after country...
> Country he look after you.'

In the two hundred or so years that whitefellas have lived upon the vast continent of Australia, it seems that we have shown little understanding of the country that we all share, let alone our fragile planet. Indeed, unless we can all learn from those wise old folk such as Bill, who maintained a harmonious relationship with their land over thousands of years, then our time here may well be limited...

\*\*\*

One day, Old Man asked if Jamie and I would like to take him out to Cannon Hill, where he used to live, to see some paintings and the country where he grew up as a child. He didn't have to ask twice!

The next day found the three of us in my truck bumping along a track that bordered a huge floodplain, parking in the shade of a huge sandstone outlier beside a rippled billabong where red waterlilies nodded in a gentle breeze.

Old Man raised his head, and pushing out his lower lip, pointed in the direction of a cave entrance hidden behind some overhanging vines.

'You go look, two lady there,' he rumbled.

Jamie and I pushed aside the vines, and crept into the darkness within. Above us upon the cool stone wall, painted in white ochre, was a female figure made of concentric circles, pulsing with energy. Nearby, in the gloom, another figure with two babies in its belly.

What stories were hidden here in the darkness among these rocks worn smooth with the feet of passing centuries? Old Man remained silent, and then motioned for me to drive on a little further. Beside the billabong a mushroom-shaped rock gave shade to shallow dimples ground into the sandstone to hold pools of ochre for the paintings that peered down at us from the ceiling above. Over the millennia folk would have sheltered under there and watched the summer storms stalk across the vast floodplain while below them the rattling waterlilies waved in the wind.

We left there an hour later to take Old Man home, for he was tired from the journey. Around the fire that night, silent in our thoughts, so many questions tugging at our sleeves, we hardly talked at all.

\*\*\*

I waited weeks and weeks for a call from Jacob, but still none came. Behind the Training Camp stood an imposing sandstone outlier where, underneath an overhanging cliff, there was a sheltered space with paintings upon the walls. I went there one afternoon to sit below the paintings and ask the old spirits that surely lived there for some help. Time was slipping away from me like sand through my fingers, and still no work done.

Three days later I spotted a pretty girl nonchalantly walking down towards the Training Camp. Thinking she was a tourist, I approached her to ask if she was lost.

'No,' she replied with a tight smile, 'I'm fine, thanks.'

She told me she was staying nearby in one of the Ranger's houses while they were away, and that she was working with George Chaloupka, an authority on Aboriginal rock art, who was writing a book on the life of Jacob at his request. Surprised, and somewhat bewildered, I asked her if I might meet George to find out his plans.

That evening with George I realised that the bird had flown, but I had to accept that he knew most of the characters in Jacob's story, and was a far better choice to write it than I. Nevertheless, I had wasted a lot of time here. So, it was time to go.

Before I left I went round to Old Man Bill's house to say goodbye. He could see that I was upset and told me to sit down beside him on his bed. I explained to him that I had been waiting all this time to work with Old Man Jacob, but that fella had changed his mind and instead had chosen to work with someone else so, sadly, now I would have to leave as I had no reason to stay in this country.

Bill was silent for a while, deep in thought, and then he turned to me.

'Hmmm,' he said, 'you got tape recorder?'

PROLOGUE

'Yes, of course, Old Man.'

'Right then,' he said with a sigh, and then turned to me with a grin.

'I tell you story, eh!'

I was too flabbergasted to reply. Never in my wildest moments had I thought I might work with Old Man Bill!

Then he said something which really floored me:

'I been waiting for you. You been waiting for me.'

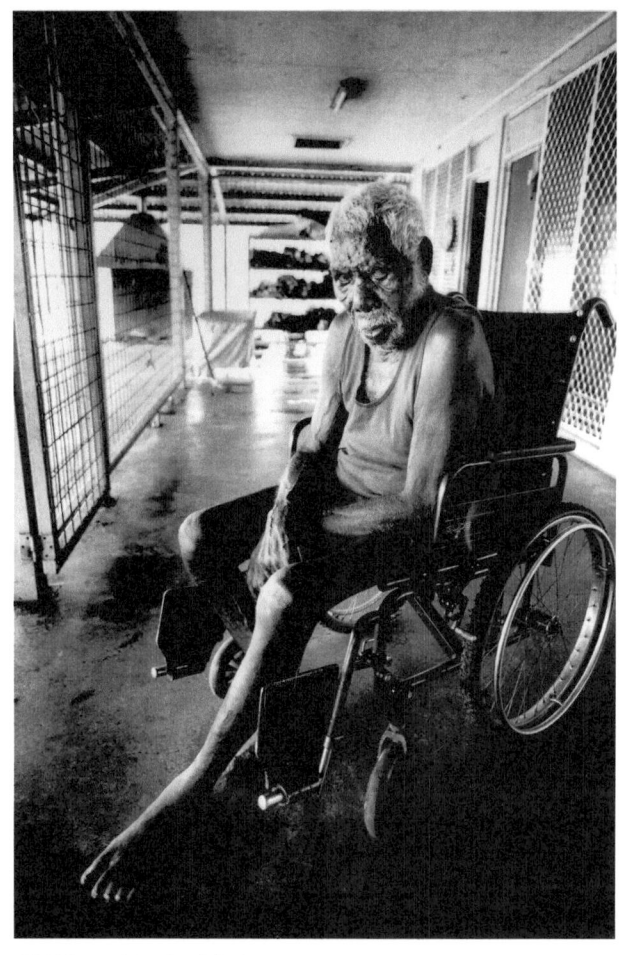

Old Man in his wheelchair.

PROLOGUE

When I had collected myself sufficiently to say goodnight to Bill, I went home but couldn't sleep, I was far too excited, so I rode up and down the road to Ubirr on Trevor's pushbike for hours by the light of the moon. Some days before I had sat in an art class with Aboriginal painters from across the river and they had shown us how to use their traditional materials: charcoal, ochre, even how to make a paintbrush out of a grass stem. Once I started painting, with no thought in my mind, I found myself drawing two hands, one black, one white, reaching out towards each other in front of a hopeful sun. It was the symbol of a dream I have had for years; a dream I believe we all share, deep inside. Now was my chance to bring this dream into reality, to work together with Old Man and hopefully place some of the wisdom of his people within a book, for the good of us all.

Several days later I collected Old Man from his house with his great-grandson Ricky, who was only four years old, but a constant companion to him; like a little Old Man himself. Together we bumped along the track back to Cannon Hill, with Ricky in the middle, to park in the shade of a friendly tree, out of the sun and the wind, in front of a cave where Bill used to camp as a child.

Above us there towered a sandstone cliff; an excellent place to camp in the Wet Season, for here were caves in which to shelter, high above the flooded plain.

I set up the microphone on the quarter-light of the truck in front of Old Man. I let him gather his thoughts, and when he was ready, pressed the Record button.

# THE FIRST STORY

## OLD MAN'S STORY

Chicken Hawk Massif.

This Chicken Hawk Rock, this one, very high.
Little cave there.
I used to camp there by myself, my mother, my father, uncle and auntie, through the Wet.
We used to eat plum, red apple; so alongside me here plenty apple tree growing.
I don't know if any of these here going to be good one; too early yet.

THE FIRST STORY

But this Chicken Hawk, in our Dreamtime story, Chicken Hawk
he done all this.
He fly over and he said, 'These people going to stay here.'
Because those days they were without houses.
Billabong, he built billabong, and he built a big mob rock there, right on top.

He used to get many fish, afternoon or night, might be fifty, seventy.
He had family with him.
And after, Aborigine people, clan, they took over, and done a few painting.
They seen it, and they built up, little by little, how this man been drawing.
So, we still doing it, and teaching young.

## OLD MAN'S STORY

I don't know, this painting, might be twenty years time, they might save him.
Might be not, because other things spoil him.
They told me everything, so I always look after here.
All my grandchildren here, my son here.
I told them, 'You stay, look after.'

Before, long time ago, when missionary was there, 1927, I was at school.
I used to come weekend here, no boat, but we used to swim.
No crocodile those days, they few.
These days full of crocodiles, you can't swim.
My cousin Bobby, we used to camp here together, but too much fight.
He used to fight fight fight, he never play good.
So I left here.

This country, I was here twelve years, ten years with my father and mother.
They gone now, my father first.
My mother she been go here to north.
So I was follow her to bring her back.
But she didn't like, she said, 'No, I was too long here.
You stay,' she told me.

Alright, I stay here, children, grandchildren they was little.
I stay here.

But before, with my father and mother, we had to go hunting.
We used to get long-necked turtle, or might be little bit of yam.
Might be little bit lily, and nuts.
Fruit for us, red apple and all the plums.

So, we following this story, keeping, telling people.
Telling youngfellas to look after in your feeling.
They put paint and they told us, those old people.
'We'll be going, you'll be look after.
Don't rub it off.'
So, we look after.

Any tree we used to chop down, oh! big argument, fight.
They would growl us.
'That tree, you chop him down, he like yourself.
Because, the world made for us.'

You know yourself what happen in the city.
We same way, but money spoiling.
White people lucky, eh?

We didn't worry about that, because we never live on money.
We was working buffalo.
Old people, they used to get meat, that's all.
Little bit of tea and sugar.
No pay money, none.
No matter what place, all been same.

Now, little bit money, they getting a little bit money.
Too much argue.
Me, I said, 'No, don't argue, because, well, because no good.
You only get nothing for it.'

Keep him this story, this story what I'm telling.
Because he good for you.
But newspaper story, lot of argument.
Where to go, what you want to do?

You might fly anywhere with a plane if you get sick of it.
But we, we can't.
We got no place in city.
We got to stay one place here.
We own this land, cost nothing.
We got little bit houses.

That enough for us, you know.

## OLD MAN'S STORY

This story, he was up there.
That high rock here, he cut it half and half, made three way.
This one, two other one, number three behind.
And we can't go across, because he stop us.
He said, 'You not going jumping there, because long way down.
Someone can jump across, he might go down.
We can't get him.'

That way, he wanted it himself.
Well, he got wing, he can fly, but we, we can't.
Look like he punish us.

Children, they climb here.
I was here every afternoon, I used to climb there.
Few yam behind, my son Jonathan, he's camping there, Chicken Hawk.
That next one, old lady there, has another name.
But I won't put that, I just put in this Chicken Hawk.

People working there.
Maybe they been working this morning.
If you keep him clean, he good too.
I seen it yesterday.

Might be story, story good for you.
Land good for you.
Some green grass, some little tree, young, growing.
That tree growing, he was growing before.
I was growing that little stick there, tree.
I never break that tree, they used to belt me.
'He'll grow, grow with you.'

That wattle tree there, he was little.
He grow now like big one.
Now good shade.
I can look that.

Anyway, old people, they didn't want to play with that tree,
play with grass or rock.
They said it's no good.
You doing it to your body.
You doing it to your father, or your uncle's skeleton.
People don't know that.

Don't play with it, you play with a dead body, or skeleton.
Bad for you, you might get bad, bad sick, and I believe that.
You know, it's true alright.
We never played around.
We used to climb and sit down quiet.

Like, you up there, you get stone, you throw down here.
No, we never do that.
They was watching us, growl us.
They said, 'No, you can't drop stick, throw down rock.
Rock will go down there, little bit long.'
So we used to leave him.

I went one time there to look, teach children.
Teach my son Aborigine life, teach him how to look after.
How to look after yourself, and kids.
He alright, sometime he go look.
Sometime he don't like.

Smooth rock, all smooth top.
But you can't walk around there, too far down.
And behind these bushes, long way down behind, no good.
You can't go there.
Business was there, ring place.
So we been block him.
I blocked him.

## OLD MAN'S STORY

Cave good, we used to camp.
Stock boy they used to come work, here we came.
Missionary and stockmen.
Twelve stockmen, they used to watch him with bullock.
And all gone now, bullock.
They gone shoot 'em, finish him up.
No good, eh, bad luck.

They ought to leave meat for us.
But no, they never think about that one.
Bullock is alright.
But buffalo little bit nuisance, you know, breaking things.

We used to camp here.
Sometimes ceremony here.
They used to have ceremony, old people.
They used to make plenty fire, good corroboree.

Nobody doing it now.
No more tree, no more growing.
They clean up.

*Did you go through Law here, Bill?*
Yes, behind there.
When we finished, we used to come here.
Big ceremony business, I mean, big one.
Might be two hundred people.
They used to make that business good.
They had good one.
All ladies separate, they used to have another ring place.
Old people another ring place.

Rivers, plenty rivers alright.
They used to swim, get file snake, long-necked turtle, and fish.
But this time you can't, crocodile there.
Everybody frightened.
Might be he'll finish, crocodile kill him.

# THE FIRST STORY

We used to cook there.
We used to come in here without fish or anything.
I said, 'If you take meat there, mosquito too much.'
So we used to leave them.

Lie down paperbark, no blanket.
Grass or paperbark.
But good Wet Season, fire, good.
This time blanket without fire, no good.
Little bit, you know, cold, you can feel him, and wind.
Fire, no trouble, that's the one we use.
But this time, all changed.
Old people all gone.

I used to camp here, Cannon Hill other side.
They used to camp out there, and Ubirr.
And other mob about Jabiluku, few caves halfway, they used to camp.

Some along Field Island, but I dunno how they used to live.
Mosquito, big jungle there.
They used to get him turtle, crab.
This time they use boat.

Dugong, they used to get him by hand.
Bring him round other side and eat that meat.
Stingray, fish by hand.

This time no good now.
Change might be, too many cyclone, all change.
I don't know, but I look meself, every place changing.
Even here, he change, no good.
Before beautiful, all the green different.
But this time no.

## OLD MAN'S STORY

We used to eat that red apple, white apple, billygoat plum, cherry plum.
Every plum we used to eat, in January might be.
All that tucker, our tucker.
Yam, goanna, sometime wallaby, sometime porcupine.
Sometime file snake, long-necked turtle.
All that easy one.
But wallaby, very smart that.

*What sort of lady was your mother?*
Solid woman, I mean she alright, good size, but tall.
She bin fight anybody.
Yeah, cheeky woman, that.
She bin belt me, see stick, big one.
I used to play, you know, something she didn't want —
She used to belt me straightaway.

Come up tea, late, get hiding.
And without eat, no dinner.
'You can sleep, no dinner.'

Late I used to cry, punish woman you know.
No tucker, she never give me.
Still breakfast she got up, and finish.

My father used to shut up.
I used to ask him something to eat.
'You listen to your mother.'

*Was he a big man like you, Bill?*
Yeah, solid man.

*And your mother, she was up on the coast?*
Yes, my mother, she gone beach.
She been stop.
She didn't like to come back.

*What do you think are the important things for your people to remember from the old days?*
They won't get it, I think, some of them.
I'm starting, long time I'm starting, twenty year to explain.
All run away.
My two daughters, son, they run away.
Now spoil beer, and everybody got TV.
Spoil.
They ought to leave him alone.

Old people, they used to burn this dry grass, they didn't worry.
Because they used to say if you keep him dry, too hard for tongue.
Young wallaby, good one, and right.
Even buffalo.

All the snake, they used to handle him.
My father used to handle him.
Used to get him and come and eat, too good.
But me, I can't.
I don't like getting snake.
No good.

*What's your favourite tucker, Bill?*
Goanna, or long-necked turtle.
Good one.

*So, in the Wet Season this would all be under water?*
No, dry here. I been sit down here, good one.
I been build meself paperbark.
Good house, but I burn it, leave him open.
You can build what you want, stringybark alright.
But they been give me caravan, houses.
So I burn it that paperbark house, good one too.
When they burn it grass, he gone, he got fire.

## OLD MAN'S STORY

Old lady there, one little house, they been build, he still there.
But mine paperbark, he finish.
Old lady, my sister, finish, she been died, poor thing.
She used to cry for me, cry, cry, and she been died.

*Was she young when she died?*
Old, old, she been long time, getting too old.
Too much drink, I think.
She would have been sit down, but other woman push in fire.
Burn herself.

*So days when you were a youngfella, you'd be out hunting every day, would you?*
Sometime every day, sometime second day.
We used to have something, meat there left, we stay one day.

*Would there be dancing and singing in the night times?*
Yes, I used to sit and watch them, little boy.
They told me, 'You got to keep him, this corroboree.'
But all dead, I can't help it.
Tape recorder alright, anything, but wrong.
You should have your own corroboree, didgeridoo, eh?

*And would there be spirits living around here from those old people?*
Yeah, might be they here.
You can hear clap stick, didgeridoo sometime.
But too many noise.

Rock, this one, sit down on top, there, oh, beautiful.
No mosquito in the night.
But you climb, come back down alright.
No more now, but I used to climb quick.
I used to climb over there.
This time I can't now; I slide down on rock.

*Did you used to go up there night time sometime, in the moonlight, sit on top?*
Yeah, too smart me, I used to climb there moonlight, no mosquito.
They used to growl me,
'What for you sit down there?'

'I like him.'

'Come down. Stay.
You stay, you nuisance.'

'I never nuisance, I just go look country.'

'Alright, and don't be nuisance.'
They used to frighten over falling down.

I said, 'No, I know what I'm doing.'

One time my father he was looking for me.
'You might fall down.'

'I'll be alright.'

I dunno, old people, they nuisance.
Next time they never let me go.

. . . . . . . . . . . . . . . . . . . .

Old Man was sounding tired; the intervals between his sentences becoming longer and longer as he gathered his breath to speak.
    'How you going Old Man, you alright?' I asked.
    'Might be I finish now. Next time might be more better,' he said quietly.
    'Right, we finish then.'
    I turned off the tape.
    After what Old Man had told me I was intrigued to know more about this place he had brought me to. So, as Ricky had crept into the back of the truck and was fast asleep on my swag, snoring peacefully, I asked, 'May I have a look at the cave, Old Man?'
    'Yer, sure, you go look. My handprint there when I was kid, like this one Ricky.'
    I crept out and walked across a large clearing into the mouth of a cave sheltered by a huge overhanging cliff. Many paintings covered the walls, some almost fresh, some only faint. People had dwelt here over a very long space of time. I searched the wall and found what I was looking for, down low, near the floor, a tiny child's handprint stencilled in white ochre, like a little signature upon the rock.
    I stared at it for a long while, my mind fixed on a day long ago.

Outside was a large clearing, surely a place of ceremony. I tried to picture the scene that must have been here once; a large fire burning into the night as figures of dancers moved around the flames, the ring of clapsticks and the drone of the didge echoing as their shadows played upon the walls of the canyon, the dust from their feet mingling with the smoke as sparks from the fire carried up to the stars.

All in the gaze of a small child, watching.

A gentle breeze whispered through the leaves that covered the arena, and now only birdsong echoed around the walls. All was quiet.

Silence fell upon me too.

I was too overcome by what I had seen and heard, simply nodded and smiled at Old Man when I returned to the truck. We drove back to the house with hardly a word spoken between us, just a wave of thanks.

But we had begun his story.

Where would it go to next?

# THE DRY SEASON

OLD MAN'S STORY

Catfish Creek in the smoke.

THE DRY SEASON

It was now August. We were in the midst of the Dry Season and everywhere the air was filled with smoke from innumerable fires lit by the Park Rangers. Their purpose was to minimise the amount of flammable material which might catch fire and rage uncontrollably through the country during the lightning storms of the following Wet.

The local tribes had been burning-off country since time immemorial, for by doing so, they eliminated the impenetrable thickets of speargrass that grew taller than a man, and thereby made it easier to pursue the elusive game that they relied upon for food. A further benefit lay in the fact that where the country had been burnt, new grass would soon spring up, and that would attract the game to come and graze the fresh green shoots where the tribesmen waited nearby with their spears.

I would wander the country close to the East Alligator River in the early mornings when the sun shone through veils of smoke, hunting for pictures. Later in the day I would look after Ubirr.

Trevor's other employee, Ian, had been offered another job — one which he couldn't refuse — and so someone else was required to look after surveillance of the art sites. The Rangers had decided that I was a suitable replacement as I knew Bill, I knew a little about his country from what Old Man had told me, and, as I was working with him, I had no plans of leaving. And so, for five hours each day I found myself in a green Ranger's uniform with a hat, two-way radio, a water bottle, and a large pair of boots in which to do my rounds. My job was to ensure that nobody damaged the natural features at Ubirr, especially the rock art, and so each hour I would walk the entire art site, keep an eye on things, and answer as many questions from the tourists as I could. I was looking after Old Man's country for him. It was as pleasant a job as you could wish for, and the wages came in handy too. However, I still found it hard to get used to the idea of looking into the mirror each morning and seeing a Ranger looking back at me.

Ubirr was a large complex of sandstone outliers where Bill's people had lived for many thousands of years and left evidence of their habitation in those innumerable paintings upon the walls of their caves and rock shelters. At the summit of the largest outlier was a lookout with warm rocks to sit upon, and here the eye wandered the green of the floodplain below with its sparkling billabongs, the East Alligator River snaking into the hazy horizon between the distant massif of Cannon Hill and the vast cliffs of the Arnhem Land plateau.

Every evening hundreds of folk would gaze upon the scene and fall into silence, for it was easy to feel that tribal people had dwelt here forever, and that this had been their home. Below the lookout black cockatoos would slowly fly by on their way home to roost in the nearby treetops, while a crowd of magpie geese, honking to each other down upon the mirror of the billabong, might suddenly erupt into flight as a dingo or two stalked an agile wallaby through the long grass of the floodplain.

It was a place be quiet, to watch and to let the mind wander.

I would wait until the sun had set and the sky let fly its final colours, and then tell the visitors that it was time to go, it would be dark soon. I'd escort them off the summit and back down to the car park where I would lock the gates and leave the place to the peace of the night.

When I was out of uniform I could return to being a photographer again. I felt that part of my job as a photographer would be to illustrate the sheer poignancy of Old Man's situation, for while he was still a child the twentieth century had arrived in his country in the form of the buffalo shooters. His father had worked for Paddy Cahill, one of the most successful shooters, hunting and skinning the beasts and being paid in sugar, tea and tobacco.

Nowadays Bill's people had left their traditional ways and followed an easier lifestyle where they could go down to the store and buy their food, rather than go hunting and gathering every day of their lives.

Bill passionately felt that without their traditional values his people were lost. His fear was that their beliefs, their story, represented by the Law that had been handed down to them by the Dreaming heroes, would disappear and that their culture, one of the oldest on earth, would soon be no more than ancient history.

Old Man Bill believed in the values of his 'old people', of which he was one of the last. Here was a man who held the secrets of his Law, but who had no-one that he could pass them on to, for, as Old Man said, no-one in his mob wanted to go through Law anymore.

In my time in the Park I had come across many pictures of Bill, but there was no portrait of him, nothing that depicted the sheer importance of who he was. So it occurred to me that I should take a photograph that epitomised his role as the tribal storyteller, the keeper of the flame; a picture to speak for him after he had passed on.

So, with that idea in mind I drew a layout on a large piece of cardboard showing Old Man 'telling story' to a youngfella sitting beside him by an open fire like when he was a boy and had camped with his old people and heard their stories, night after night, out there on the floodplain.

But what words should accompany such a picture?

At the summit of Ubirr, overlooking the floodplain was a National Parks sign with some of Bill's words upon it. They provided the perfect caption:

> 'My old people all dead.
> We only few left, not many.
> We getting too old...
> Young people, I don't know if they can hang on to this story.
> But now you know this story.
> Might be you can hang on to this story, this earth.'

I took the layout around to show him one evening while he was sitting on his bed in the warmth of the evening air out on the verandah, casually flicking flies with a goosewing fan. I sat beside him and explained what I had in mind.

He looked at the illustration for a long time, and then said, 'Yer, good one. We do that one. Good idea that one.'

He was still weak from a recent bout of flu so I suggested that we wait until he was feeling stronger, and then we'd take Ricky out to try and find a location, somewhere nearby. He nodded slowly, and said, 'Good one, right.'

And so started the longest photographic saga of my life.

\*\*\*

I had to wait two weeks for him to recover from the flu, then another week or so for the smoke to clear from all the burning-off. I had to hope that when Old Man was feeling up to it Ricky would be available too, as he was often away fishing with his father. And when the fish are on, the fish are on. Never mind about taking a picture...

One afternoon everything was looking good, so Jamie and I picked up Old Man and Ricky and drove to Cannon Hill to park up beside the billabong. But as soon as we arrived the wind got up, ruining the chances of our building a quiet fire. Old Man sat in the truck and frowned, shaking his head. We sat and watched the waterlilies waving in the wind for a while, but the breeze remained constant. The sun began to sink behind us; it would be dark soon, so we had better think of starting back. Ricky fell asleep.

'Moon might be good for picture,' suggested Old Man.

I thought of the complexities of shooting by moonlight, inwardly thinking that things were hard enough already. We started back through the gathering gloom, Ricky snoring in the back.

'Maybe we should do the shot on the moon,' quipped Jamie with a grin.

'Hmmm, need big mob diesel for that one,' said Bill.

The next morning I started cooking a curry, and knowing that Old Man was partial to a good Indian curry, went around to his house to see if he wanted some brought around later. He nodded, then told me a story of finding a cat's claw in his plate when he was eating curry at a Darwin restaurant. Having assured him that I wasn't cooking a cat, he agreed, but then he said, 'Might be we do some more story this afternoon?'

'Of course, Old Man,' I said, shelving all other plans.

I picked him and Ricky up after lunch, and he told me to drive around the back of the outlier that stood like some vast ship among the trees near his house, to the overhang where the paintings were and the old spirits that I felt had helped me earlier.

I lifted him out of the truck to sit upon the ground, Ricky beside him, while I set up the microphone and waited for him to prepare his thoughts.

He sat quietly, slowly crushing March flies with a finger into the dirt. Then he looked up at me, and nodded.

## OLD MAN'S STORY

Alamangere cave.

I'm here at this place, the name of this rock here is Alamangere.
Me and Ricky.
I'm going to teach him, you know, he look what doing.
So that's it.
Few painting here, where old people was camping.
I used to come hunting and camp here, you know, nice to camp.
Wasn't any tourists, or people, so we was quiet.

In the night they used to take dog, find possum, bandicoot or porcupine.
That's the food we used to eat.
And morning they used to go hunting bush honey.

We used to go down floodplain and get long-necked turtle,
frill-neck and blue-tongue lizard.
We used to eat that animal because that our food.
They used to make ironwood spear to get one barramundi.
No fishing line, no fish wire.

Before now, missionary came here.
Well, he teach little bit wire.

## OLD MAN'S STORY

Yes, we used to camp here, only fire.
No light, no anything.
That's all we used to eat for long time, old people.

But I was little boy.
They never get fish from river, because fish too big.
I mean you get fish now because you use line, before nothing.
Little bit of net, that was good, one or two enough, that's all.
They used to put it away then.

People didn't know about white people coming in here.
They used to just camp out anyway.
Only fire he save us.
No blanket, no sheet, no anything.
Paperbark sometime.
We used to make paperbark to leave on top, just like mattress.
Make him dry.
Rain used to come down.

Stone spear they used, that's all, knife, bit of rock.
They used to cut him fish, stone axe.
That's all we used to live on.

Anyway, story, story every night used to go on and on.
Teaching how you want to live.
'By yourself,' they used to tell me.
'You won't see your father and mother.
And you won't see us.'

This day important, important to our people.
They should keep him this one.
Because, my grandma used to explain to me, and my father.
'Because time, time for me.
I got to leave you behind.'

Uncle, I used to blame uncle, ha!
He say, 'What you want to do?'

'I'll see my uncle and auntie.'

'No, they won't be there.
That's it, only yourself.

'You might find him, your friend, somebody.
Now we, we buried in the earth.
This, our mother.
Keep that story, this earth.
Hard, hard for you.
Keep him all the time.
Don't forget.

'And the Moon, moonlight.
Full moon, you can see anything, and think about all this story.
Moon will help you.
And we, we'll be seeing you.

'Our spirit, the Law, made for us spirit.
We got to come back see you.
You won't see us. But we'll be watching you.
What you doing?

'Good?
Well, good.

'We can help you from our feeling.
Got every different feeling now when we go.
Going away, you won't see us.
But we can see you anyway.

'Where you go? Get lost?
We can show you to go back home.
But you won't see us.'

I used to say, 'Sometime you talk to me?'

'No, the Law,' he said, 'we won't talk to you.
Only you think about it yourself, how you want to work it out.
It'll be on your mind.
And you'll be think about, ha! home this way.
I got to go back this way.

OLD MAN'S STORY

'You can get lost in these bushes.
You can go might be miles and miles, and you get lost.
Don't forget water, but you don't see water.
How you going to handle him yourself to drink water?'

'I don't know.'

'You don't know? You don't know!'

'Yeah, I don't know.'

'But you will know where billabong and spring, and all that.
Ask for, yes, you'll do it, if not, our feeling, we say, "Go back!"
You'll go back, you won't see us, you got to go back to drink water.
This time we coming to explain hard, hard way.
You got to feel him yourself.'

I said, 'Yeah, I'll be strong all the time.'

'No, sometime.
When you get old.'

'Yeah, I'll be alright.'

'No. You got to follow us.
So back, so high, you can't look.
I see you.'

. . . . . . . . . . . . . . . . . . . .

All that.
That way, I explained, but young, they don't get it.
New generation no good, nobody listen.
Old generation better.

We used to go all over the place, camping.
We used to go other side the river, get honey next day.
We used to take might be one week to camp one billabong.
Get fruit, long-necked turtle and goanna.

26

Dog, important, that why we keep him.
He can find anything.
So porcupine, used to find him bandicoot, and I said, 'Ah, good.'
They used to cook him.
Good cook.
Roasted.

So that's the way we used to live, right up here, right round this rock now.
Alamangere, over there, and Ubirr.
We used to go there, up and down, go swim across, wasn't any crocodile.
They used to swim, little net, they used to get catfish, might be little barra.
That enough.

I went bush, about sixteen miles from here, we stay there.
I said, 'What for we came here?'

'Well, you got to look where you born.'

Anyway, we went there.
I seen it, couple of rocks, posts.
This time all gone.

'Here you been born.'

Myself, my grandpa, grannie, uncle and auntie, and grandma, six.
We used to go walk, walk, walk.
We stayed there six year.
And my father said, 'You got to stay, Ubirr.'
I stay with uncle and auntie, grandma and cousin.
My father he had to go to Coopers Creek; uncle died.

He come back then.
I was sit up that lookout, Ubirr, afternoon, sunset.
I look, my father other side, Cannon Hill plain.
He was coming, wave to me, I seen him.

## OLD MAN'S STORY

And auntie said, 'Who you look there?'

I sing out, 'My father coming back!'

'Oh no, that long way!'

I see him all right, and uncle he come up.
'Where?'

I said, 'There, look, I see him, he move!'

And my uncle, he said, 'Oh Christ, you sharp eye!'
True alright.

He brought two or three goanna, cooked ones, for me.
And he brought honey home, and we stay there.
He come up, I run down.
He grab me, carry me then, outside Ubirr, coming up that cave.
We stay.

He took me back then.
Because my mother she was there, Coopers Creek.
One week, two week, she took me back.
My father, uncle, auntie, and grandma.
Halfway we camp.

Because I was mucking around, too slow, play around too late, my uncle growl at me.
He said, 'You want to come quick.'
But I used to go play, get this bush sugar, eat him all away.
That way made me slow.
Anyway, we got two goanna, and we cook that night, and auntie, she said, 'We got to go early.'

I never go early, I been sleep in, wake up, nearly nine o'clock.
Too late, my uncle gone.
He go, he went first, get couple of catfish. Cook.
He'll come back, meet us.
By the time we got there, seven o'clock.
Lazy man me, they growl me.
My mother she brought lily, and bush honey.
I had it full then.

We stay there six years.

I was working there, my mother, grannie, grandpa, uncle.
Uncle used to go get him barra, he teach me then.
He said, 'See this net here?'
He was doing net.

So he made net about ten foot.
Get couple of sticks, do them up and set him up creek.
And he told me, 'We go, look that net.'
That's all we was doing.

We went there, and I see two barra stuck inside that net.
Oh! I been scream, singing out, happy like.
We got to get them out, we had a good feed.
Catfish, honey, we had plenty, lily, and yam, long-necked turtle, everything.
We was happy.

Mosquito, we used to live cave, no mosquito, top.
Right on top for six year.
We used to go up every afternoon to get camp.
Morning we used to come down.
We used to eat fish, everything, leave him bottom.
We never take him with us.

## OLD MAN'S STORY

If I used to take him with me, my mother used to beat me.
Give me hiding, wash my fingers.

'You go swim.'

We used to go, no oil, anything, my finger.

I said, 'What for that?'

She said, 'Because mosquito, they follow us.'
This time like we cook close, close, mosquito plenty there.

Anyway, my father he come back.
He met this white man, Paddy Cahill.
We was sitting down there, waiting.
And uncle, he said, 'I better go up meself.
Leave him auntie with you mob.'
I been sit down, grandpa.

Now, my uncle he come back himself, Nardab, Ubirr.
And he find this flour and rice, sugar.
And tobacco, stick tobacco, nikki nikki, they used to call him.

My father said, 'Where's that little boy?'

'He alright.'

Big mob stockmen, they was there.
Missionary was there, Church of England, Mr Dyer, school.
So my father said, 'You better go school.'
Yes, my father he promise, in the school you go.
Two year before he pass away, I don't know what's wrong.
He buried Oenpelli, him and Paddy Cahill.
They both been get sick.

So Paddy Cahill, and Billy Johnson with my father.
They went back there outback and get cattle and horses.
Paddy Cahill he been trying to bring all the meat here.
Buffalo they was here already.
But red cattle, he brought red cattle.
Goat, sheep, camel, they couldn't make them here.
Only red cattle and horses, they brought them here.

We used to eat them, when school I went, 1926.
I left then, four year I been there.
Went north for good.
Good? No, bad.

I ought to stop, but, I get wild then.
I was about twelve years old.
I said wild, think about my father night and day.
So my mother said, 'I better take him another country.
He'll forget.'

I used to get up.
Look that tree, mark, he cut it, you know, high.
He cut it mark there, and me, bottom, two of us.
That tree still there, but mark gone.
I used to look, think about my father.
This long time, this one, he took me might be one year.
Think about my father.

And my mother she get wild.
She said, 'This boy might get worse and worse.
I better go another country.'

So we went north.
I forget then.

My uncle he come back, and he get sick again.
Auntie was there, two auntie, they been start come back there, day.
And they got this message, and two auntie they been get wild.
'We all been go other way now, and we go for good.'

Because the story, this story, they was telling me every night:
'You'll be by yourself.
You won't see your auntie, grandma, uncle, grandfather.
You won't see us.'
So I used to make sorry meself.

'You'll be by yourself.'

'What I do then?'

## OLD MAN'S STORY

'Ah, you'll be work it out.
All this story now, if you keep him, this story, all story first.
Telling somebody, help you out.'

Corroboree, all the time corroboree, other people, Maningrita mob, Oenpelli.
Every night big corroboree, dancing.
You don't see him now, corroboree, all gone, that way was worry me.

We went north, corroboree there, big mob people.
Corroboree, corroboree.
Corroboree, big mob lady, all gone.
That no good.
No more, no good.

I said, 'What for, people all finish?'

They said, 'Well, we'll be done for, us.
No matter who you are, you got to go same way.'
No good.
So I been used to it now.
Yes, well, I been beaten, eh?

## Honey

Might be I was fourteen.
'Give me that axe,' I said.

'Where you want to go?' said auntie.
Good auntie, mine, they got axe from store, Oenpelli; give me.
'Where you want to go?'

'Shut up, I'll go by meself.'

'You can't even find him sugarbag!'

I said, 'Auntie, quiet.'

Uncle said, 'Leave him, let him learn now.'

'Uncle, you come with me?'

'I'm not coming with you. You go yourself.'

I been just go close, come back, empty tin, billycan.

'Where honey?'
I been shut up, like shame.
'You shamed.'

My grandpa, he said, 'You try again.
Just get him that billycan, get him that axe, and try again.'

'I can't, grandpa.'

'Go on! Get going!'

I been go, I went.
No. Come back empty.

Uncle said, 'You got him, auntie!
You see this stick here?
Morning, you got to go start looking for honey.
You come back empty, I kill you with this stick.
This stick he'll be waiting there!'

'But I can't.'

'You can do it,' he said. 'Shut up. Keep going.'

I been sleep, morning early I went.
They been teach me like bloomin' school.

'No, I'll go after.'

'Now! Because you know we teaching you.
Or you don't like, you get sick of it.
If you get sick of it, you can go away!'

Don't talk anymore; I been shamed.
I sit down quiet.
Think about what I want to do.

## OLD MAN'S STORY

'You can run away if you want.
We don't want you!'

Hard time they been give me.

'I'll take auntie. Auntie can come.'

'Yourself, you go.'

Jesus! Sit down, think about.
My mother she been sit down, quiet.

'Mummy, you take me there?'

'No. You can go yourself.'

'Grannie, grandpa?'

'No. You heard what your uncle said.'

'Auntie, we go, leave him uncle?'

'No, I can't go. Uncle been tell you.
Try.'

Go slow, and think about.
I went there.
Little rock, I was sitting down.
Just look, right round, on top rock.
I was sitting down.
Like here.

That honey was there!
I listen that honey, you know, buzz! buzz!
What's that?
I seen him close.
Honey!

I been split him axe, oh! honey!
I fill up billycan, half full.
I been happy, I go quick.
I went there, stand up.
I go, 'They might hit me.'

No, I go.
I went quick, come out, my uncle he was sleep.
'Uncle, I got honey!'
He been look.

'Good boy, do it again.
Give me that tin. You go look again, bring back properly full.
Full.
You know, this teaching, we don't teach like this.
You go.'

I went. Get honey. Full tin.
Come back.

. . . . . . . . . . . . . . . . . . .

And my uncle, he made two shovel-nosed spear.
Leave them, one side woomera [spear-thrower].

'What this woomera for?'

'You just get him. Try, try.'
I been try that spear, good one.
'You go.'

I went, uphill.
I been look wallaby, grey wallaby.
I missed him.
I been go look, everything.
I been go home, tell him story.

'See anything?'

'Yeah, I see wallaby, but why I been missed him?'

'How far?'

I said, 'Like here, and that stick, there.'

'No, you should go closer.'

## OLD MAN'S STORY

'What for?'

'What for!
That wallaby he tell you, no more long way, you missed him.
You got to go close, and bang! you get him.
You try.'

I went. Ordinary wallaby, eh! I got him alright, finish.
My uncle, I been come back.
'Here, wallaby.'

'Ah, he alright.'

Proper hard people too, they used to punish.
They never teach me like school now.
They used to teach me other way round, to get learn.
They used to growl me.

'Do it! You want to do it, or no?'

'Alright.'

So, you know, sometimes your friend, you got to tell him same story.
I had good friend, telling one another story.
That boy, probably he dead now.

Hard way.
Now we say, English way, little bit easy.
No more Aborigine people way, they tell you.
It's no good, terrible more that.
That hard way, I got him, there.

This mob answer back:
'We give you question, and you answer.'

'What for? Answer you!'

'Well, I got the answer, you know.'

'You keep your mouth shut!'

They grab me then, took me business.
Business, yeah, he hard way alright.
Properly, wicked mob I say, proper.
You got to get like that now, young fellas.
Teach.
Me, I been get trouble that one now.
Growl, growl, growl.

. . . . . . . . . . . . . . . . . . . .

Old Man grew quiet now. The three of us sat in silence for a while amidst the swelling chorus of the cicadas, the chirruping of honeyeaters, the murmur of a breeze through the surrounding trees, their leaves golden with the evening light. He looked over at me and nodded. He was done for the day.

I helped him up from where he had been sitting on the ground, for his old legs were weak now, and he climbed back into the truck with Ricky alongside him, a sleepy little boy. We drove back to his house where the rest of his family were gathered, sitting on the floor around a blaring television. I helped him into his wheelchair out there on the concrete veranda, where he stayed, away from the noise, to wave me away out into the night.

OLD MAN'S STORY

Moon shining through woollybutt trees.

The moon shone bright that night through the branches of two woollybutt trees that stood beside the campground. I looked up at that shining orb and the silhouette of the trees stretched out towards each other against the night sky, their branches mingling, and felt how they seemed to symbolise the heartfelt need for people to work together and understand each other, to be each other's witness, under the cold silver light of truth. I thought how fortunate I was to be working with Old Man here in his tribal country, and how I must help him tell his tale, for we would not have this chance together again. With that thought in mind I turned in for the night.

When I awoke the first thought in my head was that I should ask Old Man to go deeper into his story, and to hold nothing back. I found it hard to tell him this, however, for I wasn't sure how he would take what might be seen as interference, so when we next saw each other, I simply said, 'Next time you tell story, Old Man, might be good to go deeper into story, what you think?'

'Yer, might be good,' he said, with his lip pushed out in thought.

'You tell me when you want to do that one,' I said.

'Right, I think about, then I tell you.'

Two days later we returned to the cave.

## *Talking about feeling*

Talking about feeling.
We Aborigine, we say feeling of every people.
What meaning that one?

In the meaning of English, feeling is knowledge.

I know how it is when you get cut your foot.
You feel him sore, that right that meaning.
Different story, this feeling.

I got my lingo, but it's different; people don't understand.
So truth, people all over the world, they come and learn.
Feeling same, like Aborigine people.
That feeling.
You feel it yourself, myself, somebody else.

Story of school, teaching school.
That way, hard way, I get teach.
That way for hunting.
They used to make me go hunting to get something, bush honey, fish.
That's like school, eh?
Teaching.

Anyway, I went that teaching, hunting.
Get fruit, come back.
Get meat, come back.
Wallaby, goanna, all sorts of things.
We never buy any.
Now, we use money.
We pay this stuff because I'm getting old.
I can't go hunting anymore.

Those young, they should go get him my fruit.
I used to bring them old people raw fish, and get cook.
They used to sit and look me, teaching me.
Get wood, make a fire.
Big fire, cook proper.
Half cook they used to tell me:
'No, do it again.'

I know little bit of Aborigine people.
We used to go school together, Oenpelli, couple of old blokes, and cook.
What sort of a thing?

Cooking stuff, you got to learn to cook yourself.
No matter about your friend.
Might be your wife, or somebody.
You can get married, but you'll have to cook.
Follow your Law.
The Law.
That's the hard way.

Listen quiet.
I'm alongside here, teach people here.
They used to camp here, and painted.
Little bit of paint here.
What the story is, they used to sit down and remember.
Ah, I better go draw something.
That just like school, might be.

They painted here.
Wet Season they used to camp here.
Keep them dry, teaching young.

Some young, too many.
They never understand what meaning of this painting here.

## OLD MAN'S STORY

You got to look.
That mean you sit and look.
Look, and you think about yourself.
You must think about, what that painting there for?
They never telling me.
But they told me, 'You just look after, teaching other people.'

I said, 'What meaning that? What story?'

'Well, you got to save him, your world and earth and tree.
Grass, you can burn it, no matter, burn him.
But grass he'll come back again, new.
You got to keep him, that one.'

That way I keep him.
But some of them I forget.
You got to keep him, your life, painting.

Tree, you like him tree?
Yes, you look.
Good tree.
You look that tree there.
He grow when you all been sleep.
He grow there fork, and he spread out his hand.
That same there, not straight one.
All been daylight now, too late to grow.

Tree, he talking to us.
Rock, spirit there, he talking to us.
We sitting talking.
That spirit, that making him happy.
He say, 'Oh, he talking same story.'

Tree, grass, all been burnt.
You look all them plants, green again.
There's still life.
Mother Earth, our mother.
He look after us.
We look after him.

Moon he talking to us.
We talking to him.
All that piece by piece.
Little bit of story, little bit of story.

After, he spread out.
Your feeling he spread out.
Whatever your feeling is.
You come together.

You can look something, swamp, plain, rock.
How you feel?
Yourself.
That's the one he open up, you see.
He tell your body to work it out yourself.
And teach other people, other friend.
If that man might be bad man, he can't say anything, he don't like…
Well, not worth it, you wasting time.
But you might find him good man, to teach.
Sit down careful, talk one another, slow.
Point things out to one another.
That better for you.

If you can't point out, or tell one another something, not worth it.
You losing it.
But you think about kids.
They'll growl us.
We start half of it, little bit.

But this time now, we can't teach, too quick.
My time we was slow.
New generation, money and drink.
Makes them forget about our story.
That our feeling.
Story, telling story.
But spoiling now, spoilt.
I can tell that.
The easy way easy.
No good.

## OLD MAN'S STORY

You got to walk to get something to eat.
Now, we got vehicle.
Vehicle we doing little bit easy.
But you should be learn by hard way to get learn more.

Get something to eat.
The hard way more better for you to get learn.
You got to learn.
This one important.

. . . . . . . . . . . . . . . . . . .

Alright, I come to this one.
When you get married.
What sort of a man, what sort of a woman?
Might be good.
Man good, what about woman?
She should be good.
Me, I see plenty, but not worth it.
Argument.

You should keep him normal, right, quiet.
Talk with one another.
Pointing out to one another, teaching children.

If not, get that kid, take him away.
Walking around road.
Take him walk, that kid, he'll know.
You can show him anything, bird, anything.
Animal same, he'll tell you how.

There, look, we can listen one bird there.
He talking to us because we here.
He say hello, this people good.
Would have been long time, crow.
He's the manager.

One crow been here.
He come look us, what we're doing.
That old people's spirit.
They come back crow.

Bird there, he talk, you listen.
Telling us go ahead, go ahead, good.
That bird, high, rock.
Look, he's there, on top.
Because story, that story they like it.
People like him.
You like him, I like him.
Somebody should be.

Bird he gone now, he was talking, he gone.
He say goodnight, he go sleep might be.
All kind of animal come to you.
Because that mean you got story.
And they know your story.

That not really bird, but spirit.
Spirit of these people.
They was camping here, and they watching us.
To look after, might be.
Good for them and good for you.
Make you good, good feeling.

These old generation, these stories.
Not new one, no.
New one is nothing.
This one old generation, when I was kid.

Rock climbing, I used to climb and look.
Look country, plain.
I used to look, might be brolga, jabiru, goose.
Sitting down quiet, look.
That kind of thing.

## OLD MAN'S STORY

But this time, he not remember that.
Somebody don't remember this story here.
You might say, ah, not worth it.
Bad for you.
For me.
Somebody else.

You got to learn this one.
One world.
One earth.
Water, we drink each.

We look one another.
Tree, we can look.
Anything, all that.
Now little animal, snake, possum, wallaby.
Come and look you.

Sit down and talk with one another.
Think about what in your mind.
You got to think about anything, or other boy can teach.
Teaching one another.

Wind he blow, you know.
Give you idea what he can do.
Idea, give you idea.

Wind he blow, he come.
Wind same, he helping us.
Wind he got special medicine for us.
He good too.

Dingo.
Should be plenty dingo here, but all gone.
All that animal, these birds, some they talking to us.
Some I don't know, went off some way.

White cockatoo, he's the main one.
Eagle, he can tell you where's that fish.
He teach you.

Black crow, he's the boss.
Yeah, crow, he boss.
That old people's spirit.
He tell you how you happy.
Him happy himself.

Any animal, you might like him this story.
That animal, you might like him.
No one animal is no good for you.

Dry tree, that mean he dead, finish.
Like we, we'll be buried.
Life is still life.

Young.
Youngfella, he growing, like grass.
Young man or young woman.
Young lady, kid.
All that tree there growing leaf.
Young.
That way for all the kids.

Too many stories, eh?
Too many stories we don't get him.
But these go back all way.
Think about, hard, day and night.
You might pick them up, young.
I forget some of them.

But ask them.
The story, if we do that, if we losing it.
We won't get him back again.

## OLD MAN'S STORY

So we get little bit now.
If we get him little bit more bigger, he'll grow.
But nobody, nobody helping me.

Because other way you can't do.
You can't.
Be hard.
It'll be hard and hard, no good, not worth it.
You must think about all this, think about.
You can do it.
Somebody can do it.
Good for you.

So, business.
The business he good for you, young.
The business he'll grow you up.
You pick him up, you'll pick him up your story, whatever.
That business he good for you.
He open up your brain.

English, we all speak English.
But I not remember some.
Only my country I remember.
What they taught me.

River, billabong, rock painting, cave, look after.
But that's the one other people they don't know.
That's the one hard for us.
We can't handle him all that.

Some white men good, help us.
But some, they think about their way, that's the one.
Hard for us.
Some, they alright.

Look, tourists there.
They want story.

The serpent, rainbow serpent, we sitting on.
He under us, this ground, earth.
And rainbow serpent he listen.
He listen to us.
That our mother, earth and rainbow serpent.
Little bit of story there.

Biriwik her name, red woman.
That rainbow serpent, that woman Biriwik.

We don't think about anything, but should be.
Should be think about.
Spread him out word, everybody, black and white.

Earth, he won't shift.
And rock, he'll be million, million.
We'll be going, but rock he'll be there forever.
She done for us to make us feel better.
Good sleep, drink water, look sky, all that.

Woman, her name Warramarongee.
Man, his name Dalmana.
That man he done tree.
Woman come along.

He plant lily, long-necked turtle, blue-tongue lizard, frill-necked lizard,
red apple and white apple.
He said this good for people to eat.
They made this world, and story, and people.
That way they painted here.

If you forget, you can't make anything out of it.
Might be you forget…

## OLD MAN'S STORY

No good.
You shouldn't be.
You got to think about all this.
You think about yourself.
How you want to make him good.

Your story no good, you change him little bit.
Make him better.
People got brains; you can change him, whatever.
You can change him and think about something else.
People can do it, our people.
I know, I growl them all the time, to make them better.
But they won't listen to me.
If they listen, better.
Not for me; better for everybody, and carry on.
Carry on for kids.
I said that sixteen years ago, get teacher, help me.
Teacher never come.
I was in Jabiru, try find out to help.
No good.
Story very strong.
Very heavy, to clean things, clean you up, body.

If you want to keep him strong,
you can make little bit, little bit more.
Better to listen this story.
And while you think about it, you can write him all the way.

If you're good, you might find to open my story.
Might open yours, to think about.

Letter, don't read it.
Book, don't read it.
Book they give me headache too, book.
I forget some of them, more better leave them.
And listen.

Story for anybody, no matter who.
Same way, same story.
If you like him, you like him.

But story old people, old generation.
That they been draw for us.
World they been draw.

That rainbow serpent Ubirr, that's the one now.
We should look, everybody, and teach children.
Might be too late.

So this, this the one story.
If you wanted to think about, anybody, and make it.
Try write him out yourself.

. . . . . . . . . . . . . . . . . .

# THE FIRST SHOOT

It was late September and the days were unrelentingly hot and dry, with a quiet spell in the middle of the day when it seemed as if everything in the bush had crept under a rock and gone to sleep. I was working three days a week at Ubirr keeping an eye on the art sites, and also keeping an eye on the country for any sign of fire which I would have to report over the radio. However, the air was clear; nobody was burning off anymore as the country was tinder-dry. As there was no smoke around and the visibility was much better, it seemed appropriate to think about taking the photograph of Old Man Bill 'telling story'.

I caught up with him one afternoon at the Border Store where he was sitting at one of the outside tables sheltering underneath a beach umbrella signing copies of his books, surrounded by some shapely Canadian girl tourists. Even though he was in his eighties he was still very attracted to the opposite sex and relished being in the company of women, especially pretty girls who he liked to tease, and with a wicked glint in his eye ask them to come and sit beside him.

These Canadian girls sat spellbound as he told them of days past when he would go 'walking the country', maybe up to Cobourg Peninsula where his

## OLD MAN'S STORY

mother lived beside the sea, or down south to Katherine; journeys of several hundred kilometres, barefoot.

The girls shook their heads.

'That's a long, long way,' one of them said admiringly.

Old Man shrugged.

'Just take few days, might be. Didn't wear no clothes then, just take couple of spears.'

Another asked if there had been any close encounters with crocodiles.

He shook his head. 'Me too dark. They like you whitefella,' he grinned.

Here Old Man was in his element: telling stories.

Watching him at that table surrounded by a spellbound crowd only firmed my resolve to ensure that any picture that I took of him would have to convey the impression that here was the storyteller; someone who had a tale to tell that all of us could learn from.

The girls rose to leave, shook his hand and waved to him as they drove away. He asked if I would drop him back home, so I helped him out of his wheelchair and into the truck, and with the wheelchair up on the roof rack drove back to his house.

'Old Man, you want to do that picture soon?' I asked.

'Yer, tomorrow night might be good,' he growled, 'Ricky he there, house.'

'Fine with me, Old Man. Good picture, you and Ricky together, telling story.'

'Good one,' he nodded, 'moon he good too.'

Indeed, the moon was nearly full. So it was settled; we would shoot the picture the next evening, outside the cave where Old Man had told his story. Everything was fine, there was no wind. Old Man was in good health, and Ricky was available. It should have been easy.

I picked them both up from the house the following evening as the sun was sinking and dusk was settling on the day. It had been a hot one too. I had been working up at Ubirr all day and was pretty tired, and therefore not as mentally prepared as I should have been.

Ricky wasn't too sure what was going on. At this time of day he should be sitting down to supper with the family, so he was bewildered as to why he was being taken away. He was only a little boy, he'd never had his picture taken before.

We arrived outside the cave, and Old Man staggered on his walking stick to sit down on the ground while I scrabbled around looking for sticks to make a fire for them to sit around. But by the time I had a decent supply it was nearly dark and the moon was already up. There was no time to waste, the moon would be out of the picture soon, so I ditched the idea of having a fire, which was just as well because the surrounding bush was so dry that a runaway spark could have started a blaze. I scampered around like a scalded cat setting up the flashlight instead. This had to be run from a generator connected to the truck's battery, and as the leads weren't that long, the truck had to be brought really close to the scene and the engine kept running to maintain an even charge. I reversed the truck so I could move it in tighter, crashed into a tree with a bang, and then drove right up to both of them.

Ricky was sitting in the glow of the headlights and he was looking decidedly alarmed. What the hell was going on?

I turned the modelling light on for the flash and the scene didn't look too bad at all, so I set the camera on the tripod and backed away to frame the picture. The problem now was that neither Old Man nor Ricky could see or hear me, for I had totally disappeared into the relative gloom beyond the reach of the light, and my voice couldn't be heard above the sound of the chugging diesel.

I emerged from out of the darkness and told Old Man to just chat away to Ricky as if he was telling a story, and returned to the camera, back into the dark.

Ricky was looking around for where I had gone.

I ran back into the shot and told Ricky just to look up at Old Man as he spoke to him. Fine!

Back at the camera, everything was looking good until I pressed the trigger. The sudden flash startled both of them. Old Man was used to this kind of thing but Ricky was visibly alarmed. By the look on his face Old Man might have been telling him a really scary tale and it took quite a while before Old Man could calm him down.

I carried on to the end of the roll, but in my heart I knew that the shot lacked any credibility whatsoever. I tried another roll with Old Man on his own but he looked a bit lost sitting there in the night with nobody to talk to, so I called a halt to the session.

Ricky was asleep in the back of the truck by the time I packed up. I helped Old Man back into the seat, and when we returned to the house Ricky awoke groggily, climbed out of the cab and ran to the arms of his mother. Old Man climbed into his wheelchair out on the verandah, shook my hand and said gently, 'Thank you, my friend.'

'No, thank you, Old Man, we got picture, but I don't think he's much good.'

'Yeah, right,' he grunted.

Later, I sat outside in the moonlight under the branches of the two woollybutt trees and resigned myself to the fact that we'd have to try again.

I sent the rolls of film off to a lab in Melbourne who sent me back the proofs days later, and the shots had come out better than expected, but certainly not good enough.

I took them around to Old Man to show him. He put his glasses on, tied behind his head with a piece of string, and peered down at the shots for a long time, saying nothing. Then he came to the shots of himself, sitting on his own.

'Hmm, I reckon me look too skinny, eh?'

And he did, too; he certainly didn't look the man of stature that he was.

'I'm sorry Old Man, they're just not good enough.'

Silence.

'Can we have another go?' I asked sheepishly.

'Hmmm,' he rumbled, and then nodded.

'Might be moonrise, next month, Old Man?'

'Yer, he alright, no matter.'

I breathed a sigh of relief.

He looked up at me.

'Might we do some more story, eh?'

'Of course, Old Man, tomorrow alright?'

'Yer, good one,' he nodded, 'see you tomorrow.'

THE DRY SEASON

Old Man and Ricky.

## OLD MAN'S STORY

Sunrise over Nardab Floodplain in the early mist.

This story we talk about to look after country...

Look after country.
Because that Dreamtime, old people, our people, had a few painting.
This way they draw, they never think about anything.
Only sit down one place, and look after this country.
This Kakadu now, they used to come round and look after.
That way they teach me.

THE DRY SEASON

They were telling me,
'Better look after country.'

I said, 'Why?'

'Because you love your country.
You got to love it yourself.
It's your country, you know, this world.'
Anyway, these all Gagudju people here.
They used to look after this country.

## OLD MAN'S STORY

This time now, youngfellas, I don't see anybody.
Might be they don't like it, or they won't talk about it.
Or they forget, or know too many things.
But too many things, you got to be think about this.
And look after.
Look after, no matter what.

Grass, tree, rock, rock painting.
Any wallaby, you look after.
They used to kill him before, but leave him half.
They never kill him all lot.
Anyway, emu, brolga, they was look after.

On the plain there, Nardab, buffalo, big mob.
That time I been growing.
I was ten or eleven years old.

They shooting buffalo for that Paddy Cahill.
My father he was working, and same time he look after country.
Used to go place to place in the billabong.
The buffalo they used to come down, shoot, skin.

A buffalo skin might be worth money.
We didn't know, old people didn't know.
Might be worth money, white man.

Old people never get anything out of it.
Only bit of sugar and tea, little bit of tobacco.
And you know the country, people look after each.
They give little bit story.

And my father he think about.
He said, 'Hey, how about your story?'

Paddy Cahill, he said, 'No, I dunno.'
They been argue there outside Ubirr.
'I don't know this, I know buffalo, I want skin.'

I been grow.
I used to stay beside my father.
He was pointing that Ubirr lookout.
And he said, 'Son, don't forget that you got to be look after.
People, might be they coming.'

I said, 'What sort of a people?'

'Ah, I won't tell you.
You will know yourself.
Just look after country, for us.'

'Well,' I said, 'Daddy, we teach one another.'

He said, my father said, 'I won't be with you.
I'll be gone.
You'll be by yourself.
Now you think about, you will?'

I said, 'Might be.'

He said, 'Don't say that!
You got to look after country.
What about big mob people, they'll come, what you do?'

I said, 'What kind? Aborigine?'

And he said, 'This mob now, might be.'

My grandpa, he was alive yet.
I said, 'What idea my father?'

He said, 'These white people now.
You going to be talking to yourself.'

'Then I get another youngfella?' [to take through Law]

'I dunno, they won't come with you.
They won't talk with you.'

And that true, fifteen year now.
Still no youngfella with me.
They walk away from you.

## OLD MAN'S STORY

He remember, my grandfather, and father, and uncle.
That's the one I'm talking about, painting, must look after.
This little cave that old people was here camping.
They draw snake and fish.
I can look inside there.
But running down this water here, he might spoil him.

This tree here, white apple.
White apple good eating, this big one here,
I dunno any fruit, no.
Little bit of yam here.
They used to travel to Cannon Hill Pass to get yam there.

Auntie, old lady, these people been camp here, here that red lily fruit.
They used to eat that.
In the night they used to take a dog, get bandicoot or porcupine.
They used to get a bag full, and roast it in the morning.
Good eating.

Daytime they used to go get goanna, frill-necked lizard, blue-tongue,
file snake, long-necked turtle.
Short-necked turtle, might be.
They used to eat, some of them.
I never eat any, I don't like him short-neck.
Long-necked turtle alright.

And pine, pine tree this one, that good tucker.
Nobody using it now.
We used to cook him all day, good eating.
Skin, they used to chuck him in water.
In the morning taste like sugar, like tea, we used to drink.
Honey, plenty honey here, but nobody getting it.
Youngfella doesn't know, youngfellas they don't know.
And I say look after, listen story this. I'm looking after this one, Ubirr.
I made two books to look that painting, draw.
So you will know yourself, all over the world.
You can look.

I'm telling you when I was young.
I stay one place, Ubirr, cave.
You people might be same way, no matter what colour.
And this story here now, you don't know.
Why?

You know plenty other things, the other thing plenty alright.
You making lot of things, video, TV.
What that for?
Anything?
You can look people there, walking around, story.
But what you make him?
You make this world look good?
Or better this old generation?

That thing I reckon he will just keep you mad.
I know you can use him, but he keep you mad.
Lot of noise.
You like it?

What about city?
What happening there?
How many people?
I'm talking this one here, but how many people there now?
How many?
Thousand, thousand, thousand people in the city.
How many cities, not one or two?
All over the world, Greek, Japanese, Indian, African, Indonesian.
Now what happening there?
Fighting.
We stay here, we don't fight each other.
That silly way to fight each other.

## OLD MAN'S STORY

Why you born and grow up?
You a man now.
The world, you can see this world.
You know all that tree name, and you getting a bullet through your body.
Why?
That silly thing, you don't like it, why?

We, ah, few boys they fight, make them silly little bit, something.
But they won't fight all the time, and shoot one another, no, only few.
Before alright, old people they used to fight.
But they said, 'No, we go too far. What for?
We kill each other, uncle and nephew and mother and auntie.'
They said, 'No, no good.
More better put it all, spear, woomera, put it down, forget.
What we do? Better to look after country, all these paintings.'

They been finished, they been sit down.

Our Law, we keeping our Law.
We telling you little bit Law, not much.
Looking after one, looking after country.
Looking after water, plain.

Fire, he can burn, fire, you know fire he burn.
What you make him, he going to make your goanna, frog, lizard.
They grow fat then.
That why old story, old people, they used to burn him grass.

Wallaby then, they used to keep him grass.
Some place for wallaby.
But too dry now, leaf, if you sneak up now, him listen.
But Wet you can sneak up might be some way.
Plenty wind, you can get him.
You can't go wind side.
You got to go behind wallaby, so he can't listen.
That's the story.

If you got spear, you can get wallaby, if you want, without noise.
Gun might be he run away.
But I dunno, you people, you don't understand that.

Sugarbag, bush honey, you can get him, if you like him.
These apple, white apple, red apple, that our fruit.
We save them, save him country; we try best.
Now, we looking after this one.

You got to eat bush honey, yam, any sort of a fruit.
Long-necked turtle, file snake, goose might be.
To build your body and give you good blood.
I know we don't get much, might be bandicoot.
Bandicoot like rabbit meat, but more better.
Bandicoot good one.

Ringtail possum, more sweet that one, and goanna.
And that palm there, that good tucker that one.
He grow little bit more, cut him bottom, cook him.
Good tucker.
We used to eat that one.
He grow big mob.

See that palm now, he been burn, eh?
But he got new leaf, he growing.
Good tucker.

That palm, leaf green.
All grass green because he been burn.
This one didn't burn, he's still dry.
That mean wallaby he got to eat that dry grass, no good for tongue.
That wallaby skinny.

Bullock, wallaby, buffalo, all same.
But wallaby more better.
Young wallaby, red kangaroo, all that, they eat grass.
Come down in the night and eat grass, make him fat, solid.
If he can't eat that thing, he grow skinny.

## OLD MAN'S STORY

Tree, he dry alright because fire.
But he'll come back new leaf, rain.
All that little piece, little piece.
That story with it.

I been travel around little bit, Alice Springs, Ayers Rock.
But in the night I didn't like him.
I used to come back here.
I never sleep much.
That's it, because I'm sitting on this one.
Used to say, 'Come back, come back.
Wrong place.'

Might be Dreamtime made for us, everybody.
But you should looking after proper.
I look after.
You should be look after.
Another man look after might be better.
Better for everybody, eh?

This earth, important this one.
Earth, we got to go to.
No matter who he is, or colour.
Our mother, this one.
World, or anybody, no matter who colour.

Rock, you can't worry this rock.
He'll be there million, million, million year.
Still there, same.
We got to go.
Rock, he can't go.

But I'm in this earth.

Well look after, even grass, seed, plants.
That young, all them leaf there, he growing.
That big tree, that mother.
And the little one, he growing there.
Little one he growing big one.

All that green, this one, grass he grow.
That young one, like that tree, father.
This one, mother.
This one, earth.
Way we got to go, we come from earth.
And that tree, same way.
He grow this.

Tree, he grow alright.
But sometime he dry, he finish.
But young one, he grow young.
All same story, no matter how.
Might be that tree, you look, this one he never grow straight.
He been grow late, any kind of tree, to tell you how to look after.

We look after, we sit down.
Shade, we like him shade.
Well, tree he can't help us in the night.
Because we move around tree, that grass he don't grow.
When we sleep, he'll grow.
Tree, he can't grow today.
Today we sit down, he can't grow.
He got to grow night, when you sleep.
You might dream, and that grass he grow, daylight he stop.
We move.
Funny, eh?

And that's it.

Tree, water, rain he come.
Cloud, that rain he come, raining.
Because wind he got special medicine for us.
He give us not much, little one.
Each people, no matter what country.
But he keep us little medicine.

## OLD MAN'S STORY

If you sit down, hot, no wind.
You'll be start looking for wind.

'Hey, where's this wind?'

Well, that's it, he got medicine.
He put water then, we drink.
We drinking water.
Well that seeing now.
He work it out.

Cave, he stay forever.
Tree, he go sometime fire, no matter.
But rock, you can't talk about rock.
Million, million year, he'll be there.
We'll be finish.

Rock, he can't finish.
He got to go, go, go.
Here, years and years.
He'll be there.

Old people, in beginning, start, this rock, they seen it.
After, we.
He's still there, he don't move.
But we, we go.
They been sleep here, old people, nowhere to camp.
So that's it.

Rock, main one, this shelter here.
More better, don't touch it, don't rub it off, just leave him.
Just look that painting, because kid, other people, they can look.
Plenty Ubirr.

How many people coming?
I said, 'Don't touch.
If you touch him, any painting, you won't see anything anymore.
Because very old.
And that painting good for you.
Tell you how you feeling, you know.'

Old people, our people, they watching us, they like it.

That way, my father, he said, 'Don't forget.
If you forget, can't be worse.'

But I said, 'If I can't look after country…'

He said, well, short — 'You got to go.
But you look after, little bit longer.
Look after yourself, and look after country.

'And all that world, big world.
No matter who people, where they come from, what they come from…
They'll come.'

Well, this one now, tourist, we say, 'Where from?'
This one he from long way.
But he take a lot of trouble to come here.

Might be Japanese.
I been look Japanese.
German, I been look Border Store, too many.
And Indian.
One Indian, I was talking to him,
I said, 'Look plain, I'll take you look plain.'

He said, 'These, these riches.
We, we finish.'

Next minute he sit down.
Cry.

. . . . . . . . . . . . . . . . . . .

We took a pause here while I turned the tape over, and lit a cigarette for Old Man to smoke while I went looking for Ricky who had spotted a wallaby in the grass and quietly wandered off in its direction. Watching Ricky stalking it through the bush I imagined Bill as a child, out there upon the floodplain with his family, learning the skills of hunting and fishing, and in a deeper sense, learning the rhythms of his country.

OLD MAN'S STORY

Ricky was hiding behind a tree watching the animal, which, hearing me, bounded off into the undergrowth. He gave me a rueful grin, then followed me back to Old Man and sat down cross-legged beside him.

There was such a special bond between these two and I was sure that a lot of Old Man's words were for Ricky's benefit, for him to hear now and to fully understand when he was older, a young man growing into his prime when the thoughts of these days spent with Old Man were but a cherished memory. With Ricky once more by his side, Old Man turned directly to him, and spoke.

. . . . . . . . . . . . . . . . . . . .

My mother, she was carrying me inside in her belly.
She carry me all over the place, hunting.
When she feel it, she quiet.
No hospital, anything.
My father he don't sleep close.
My father used to sleep long way from my mother.
Still I mourn, but still.

I was laying down.
My mother she was laying down paperbark, grass.
I was child.
I wake up in the morning, I crawl.

My father he was laying down.
'Hey, who you?' and he look me.

'I son.'

'Come on!'
He grab me.

I mean little bit change, white people hospital now.
But I been born bush, about sixty mile north from here.
We stayed there might be couple of months.
Come back Ubirr, because nearly Wet.
They made little raft, to swim across.

Might be you understand, you got story this, or forget.
When you was kid.
You didn't know anything.
I was like that, I started, just crawl, play, that's all.
Every one of us, same way.

I started talking.
They been leave me.
Leave him that little boy, let him talk.
I used to yell out, cry, any kid he can cry.
But night I never cry much.
Just go sleep.

Well this kid business, now better in hospital.
You go hospital, kid him born.
But you should keep him your Law, your generation.
Our generation to generation.
No more new way.
That for European, white.
Not for us.
Everything he come out from European.
He show you, show us how.
But you forget things.
You behind.

When you get up, you can't even get up.
I used to try to stand up, but no, I couldn't.
I used to get up, sit down, fall down again.

'Leave him,' my mother, father used to leave me.

Uncle said, 'Grab him!'

'No, let him get little bit hard, his knee.'

I used to walk, one, two, arse-over, fall down.
'Leave him.'

## OLD MAN'S STORY

I used to get up again, no more crawl.
It took might be two months, three months, I used to get up.
They been stand him up stick, put him in the ground.
They been stand him up.
I used to stand up, make him strong.
My mother used to say, 'You stand up there, make you good.'

I used to fall down again, crawl.

'Get up!'

I used to get up.
They used to growl me.
They said, 'Leave him, let him get used to it.
He got to stand up, he got to walk.'
I used to get up, I start walk, no.
They put one post like here, another post there.
They was talking to me.
I understand, but hard to pick up this word.
When you kid, you can't pick him, eh?
Yabba yabba, like that.

So, my father took posts, he said,
'You got to walk here.'

I crawl.
Used to pick him up me, go back here.

'You stand up here.'

I used to hang on, go along that tree, by that little post.
Still, I used to walk there.
My mother she never pick me up.

'Leave him.'

I been walk now.
I used to walk like here to that tree.
Fall down, cry.

'Leave him, let him cry.'

I been go might be two months.
I used to get up early now, walk around, play around.
Well, people like that, eh?
People, your people, no matter who people, who colour.
Same way alright?
Me, Ubirr, this one, that been school of me.

Soon as I been walk, long way now.
My father used to go for fish, or something.
I used to run, follow my father.
Used to pick him up me.

'Mummy,' I used to cry, 'I want to go too.'
Lot of kids do that.
He go, my father.
I used to go.

But my mother used to say to my father,
'You better start going now.
I'll take him another walk, this way.'

I been big now.
Three or four years old.
My father been go get him file snake and long-necked turtle, that floodplain.
I been walk there, run, run along my father.
He throw all that file snake.
'What for you come here?'

He took me back home.

When I been get strong, we went Cannon Hill.
Make all that fingerprint there, and footprints.
My mother used to look after me.
Make him all that grass, paperbark.
Good bed, but no blanket.
We used to cover up paperbark, no blanket.

## OLD MAN'S STORY

What I'm saying now, myself, I think about.
My mother and my father and uncle, they done good job.
They was look after me.

I been brought up now big boy, I was fourteen.
We been go across the river.
But my uncle wasn't strong, and my father.
My mother she been strong swim.

I said, 'No, you stay here, I'll swim across.'
I took that gear, leave him there.
I been come back pick him up my uncle.
Take him across, and grandpa.
Swim across other side.

I been strong.
I been come back grannie, take her there.
I been come back for father.
I been pick him up.
We been swim together there.
Crocodile he been just come out, like that ant bed there, close.

My father said, 'Go on, get out!'
Crocodile he gone, anyway.

We went walk.
'You strong alright, you done good job.'

And grannie, my grannie, she had gear, with walking stick, walking.
We been go cross that plain.
And buffalo, oh! big mob!
Two hundred, three hundred, they been run along grannie.
I said, 'Might be they'll run over her, or bump her.'
I been go back straight, straight along to my grannie.
I been grab her arm.

She said, 'What for you grab me arm?'

I said, 'Big mob buffalo! They might push you!'

We been walk.
Buffalo been split up.
They been go half and half.

We been walk creek.
I said, 'We'll stay here, Coopers Creek.'
My mother, she said, 'What do we eat?'

'I dunno.'
I don't know, what do we eat?

I said, 'Give me that shovel-nose spear.'
Buffalo, young one, I got him.
He been run, fall down.
I been sing out, 'Buffalo there, look!'

'You got him!'

We been cut him up, cook him, roast him, eat.

Early in the morning, I said, 'I'll go and get honey.'
Two billycan full.

We been travel north, we been start walk.
We been walk day like this, hot day.
We hot, old people, this is.
Well, I'm feeling meself too, hot he make me no good.
I said, 'You mob, sit down.'

I go two billycan, run billabong, get water.
I been come back, water him, make him wet.
And we been walk then, afternoon we come out beach.
Me, I could go for horse to eat.

We seen it, one canoe.
He had turtle spear, rope.
I don't know who brung her.
I been look, hey! rope, everything here.

## OLD MAN'S STORY

And my uncle, he said, 'I'll paddle him for you, don't miss.'
We been go find him turtle, one.
I been mile yet, I been get him.

That way, all these kids now.
You got to well look after, to grow.
But this time, now, people don't look after.
They just let them go, kids.
Jabiru, they walking around.
I look, make me shamed.

Mother should look, look after.
My mother she been look after me.
I been turn around, look after her.

Because I used to give her money.
My mother didn't like money.
I said, 'Hey, you was carrying me.
My turn to look after you.'

And people now, they can't do it.
White people, might be they understand, some of them.
This about, this thing now I'm talking about: kids.
Why you born, and get up, and shake your leg.
You got to walk, get stronger.

These white people, they don't care, they don't listen, nobody got him.
Because more white people than we.
But should be the Law, your story, you should keep him.
For next one kid, next one kid.

But lot of things growing another way, time, TV.
Aborigine people too, and you're losing it, your Law.
What dream, Dreaming shared, you got to grow.

See that grass he grow, tree he grow.
He shared Dreamtime story.
For people this story.
Missing.

You can do it, I suppose.
If everybody will do one way.
Might be we make him people good.

No good growling money.
Because money we don't know, only from European.
Might be this mine here he make money, for European.
But what European helping us?'
To understand.
Understand what you're doing with your money.

You can buy a car, if you want to.
But next minute you get accident, that silly.
White people same, same colour, accident.

This, the Law.
If you keep him very strong, you look after yourself.
And you save him.

Car, Toyota.
Some people they do, look after vehicle.
Because they know they got to use him, how many year.
Little bit no good, they get something.
Put him on, new one.
Might be wear out, like we wear out, too.
You got to eat tucker, to make him strong.
Toyota he drink water, he drink oil.
That tucker for him, to make him strong.

You understand why you was kid.
With your mother, with your father, grandma.
That people now, that important that one.
Keep you well look after.
What they doing now, they dying young.
Because not look after.

. . . . . . . . . . . . . . . . . . . .

OLD MAN'S STORY

That was it for the day. There was a gentle wind blowing through the trees. The cicadas had started their noisy swelling chorus as the temperature dropped, and now there was a fidgety restlessness in the surrounding bush. Ricky was tired, and no doubt hungry too, so I packed everything up, helped Old Man into the truck and took them both back to the house.

The sun was falling, but the afternoon was still warm. I felt like a walk in the bush so I set off towards a nearby paperbark forest, coming soon to a small billabong where the trees were scorched by recent fires and the sun shone golden upon the surface of the water. Old Man's words were still in my head, and, to me, there seemed such a gentle symbolism in the image of the trees, their trunks blackened by the fire, but still standing strong, in the light of the dying day.

# THE SECOND SHOOT

The weather was changing and the long Dry Season was coming to an end. The approaching Wet Season was announcing its impending arrival with mighty columns of cloud which would form into thunderheads, and the days would darken in the midst of the afternoon, lightning would flicker over the escarpment and thunder rumble from the distant walls. Sometimes there would be a scattering of rain borne upon sudden winds, but this would only fall for a short while as the storm passed over, the moisture only adding to the humidity so that the days became stickier and even more uncomfortable.

My days were changing too. The Seasonal Rangers had finished their six-month stint working in the Park, and most of them had left. Where previously I shared the day with them, working five hours a day doing surveillance at Ubirr, I now had to be there for the entire shift. Eleven long hours straight, opening the gates in the morning, keeping an eye on things all day, and not locking the gates until I had checked that every single tourist had left the place and I could go back to camp.

I enjoyed the work — talking to tourists each day and telling them about Ubirr and the people who had lived there for so long — and there was a satisfaction in having to look after the place and watch it go through its changes. It felt like it was my patch, my responsibility; like I was Old Man's gardener, maintaining this special place for him and his old people. However, this also meant that I had much less time to spend with him, and therefore less opportunity for getting that elusive photograph finally taken.

I had decided to return to our first choice for a location, out near Chicken Hawk where Old Man had taken Jamie and I to look at the paintings in the cave. Shooting there would give a sense of place to the picture: Old Man by the fire in the twilight of his days, sitting out there beside the billabong, with the full moon shining down over the distant escarpment.

The perfect moonrise — when the moon rises as the sun sets — would be on the coming Sunday, two days hence, but I was working up at Ubirr that day from morning to dusk, so the shoot would have to be tomorrow, Saturday. If I waited until Monday the whole scene would be too dark by the time the moon finally appeared, for it rises over the horizon each day almost an hour later than the day before.

Time was running out for us to get out to Chicken Hawk safely too. The first rains had fallen and the track out there skirted the floodplain. Soon it would be too soft to drive upon without getting badly bogged, and the thought of being stuck out there overnight in mosquito hell with a fragile tribal elder, probably the most important man in Kakadu, and a small child of four, didn't bear thinking about. So the pressure was on.

I explained the situation to Bill. We would have to shoot tomorrow evening, without fail. He nodded, he would be ready to leave at five-thirty, Ricky too.

The scene was set.

The day dawned clear, and the clouds held back, until the afternoon when they appeared lurking upon the horizon like sentinels, putting me into a state of siege.

Would they hold off for the evening?

Old Man and Ricky were both waiting for me on the verandah, and once aboard, feeling like celebrating, we zoomed up to the Border Store for some ice-lollies which they were both partial to. I can still see in my mind's eye those two black faces next to me slurping away at the bright pink ices as we lurched along the track through the trees that bordered the floodplain. Ricky climbed over the seat and onto my swag in the back, for the track was bumpy and he was getting thrown about somewhat.

We emerged out of the trees, and within minutes were at the edge of the billabong and stopped to look at the scene. An hour ago there were a few clouds on the horizon, but now there was a threatening stormy look to the eastern sky, and though the moon should be up already, there was no sign of it whatsoever. Old Man stared out of the window and frowned at the bank of approaching cloud, shaking his head.

'Would you be making a fire out here if that weather was coming your way, Old Man?' I asked anxiously.

He tilted his head back towards the sheltering caves behind us.

'More better back that way,' he rumbled, 'good cave there.'

From behind our heads came the sound of steady snoring. Old Man turned and looked at Ricky's soundly sleeping form.

'Huh, look like Ricky he dead man anyway.'

The sky grew darker, and then the first drops of rain fell, so I drove out of there, with flickers of lightning through the trees, back to the house. We would have to try again the next evening, for it would be our last chance at a moonrise at Chicken Hawk. By next full moon the whole area would be flooded out, the track totally impassable for several months. But I was meant to be looking after Ubirr that evening, so I would have to find someone to cover for me. Luckily, Derek, one of the part-time Aboriginal Rangers said he would fill in for me if the District Supervising Ranger, the boss, agreed to it. I went round to the Ranger's house and explained the situation. He didn't look too happy about it when he grudgingly agreed to let Derek cover for me, but said he would have to check with Old Man first thing in the morning.

I hardly slept that night tossing and turning in my swag in the back of the truck, the moon scudding through storm clouds like the thoughts dragging through my mind.

I went round to see Old Man the next morning, haggard and wired. The boss was there already, out on the stoop talking with him, and I could tell that I was the subject. The guy would be happy when I was gone out of there, for I hadn't made his job any easier, that was for sure. He jumped into his Ranger's truck and tore away. Bill waited until the truck was gone, and patted me on the knee.

'He alright, no matter.'

I said I'd be around later, at half five, just like before.

I paced around Ubirr all day like a man in a cell, up to the lookout every hour to check the sky. It was a cool clear day but by four, when Derek turned up to relieve me, the clouds were once again gathering on the horizon.

Old Man was waiting in his wheelchair out on the steps, but something in his face told me that all was not right.

'What's the matter, Old Man?' I asked with trepidation.

'Ricky he gone,' he said, 'when I sleeping, his father take him fishing Cannon Hill.'

'Let's go and get him, Old Man. We better hurry.'

If we moved fast I could pick Ricky up, for I knew the place where they went fishing. With Old Man aboard we hurtled along the track to Cannon Hill and the little group of houses there, coming to a halt outside one of them. Old Man called out to the sleepy occupants on the verandah.

'Where Ricky?'

'He gone Point Farewell. They shooting goose.'

My shoulders slumped. Point Farewell was at the mouth of the East Alligator River, four hours away. The magpie geese would be there in their thousands. Disconsolate beyond words I waved goodbye, and then drove back past the billabong to check the scene anyway. The storm clouds approached like an invading army; the moon had fled. I was almost relieved, for if it had been the perfect moonrise and there had been no Ricky, I think I would have jumped in the billabong into the jaws of a waiting crocodile. We sat in silence, the two of us, until the sky grew darker and the rumble of thunder woke us from our reverie.

It was a quiet drive back to the house. I thought, what the hell do I do now? Could we go the extra mile?

I asked Old Man what he thought, could we try again?

'Yer, he alright,' he said calmly, 'might be we do some more story too?'

'Sure Old Man. Weekend's good. I'm not working.'

'Good. Ricky he be back by then. We do some story and get that picture too.'

'Might be hard to do both same day, Old Man.'

'Yeah, too much for that little boy. We do story first, eh?'

'Then we get that picture before he go away again, hey?'

'Right.'

Days later. when I went around to the house, Ricky was there with his mother who was plucking feathers from a magpie goose. When we returned to the cave he solemnly sat beside Old Man who, this time, seemed to address him more directly.

OLD MAN'S STORY

Mushroom Rock, Nardab Floodplain.

When you grow, will you look after these paintings?
You grown now, your father he call all these trees names.
When you little, you don't know, you can't call him name.
That tree, when you grow strong, you can listen that tree.
He give you name.

Grass he got name, palm tree he got name.
All that, little piece, little piece.
But you get him together now, he big one.

Somebody he can give it to somebody.
Some story, if you want to, you don't like, well, no good.
Idea is no good.
Your feeling is no good.

Because this thing, you don't know.
Your feeling.
He don't have to be hard for other people.
Your feeling you give easy.
And you'll be easy yourself.

## OLD MAN'S STORY

Me, I've been doing this one, because they teach me.
They said, 'You got to be easy, everyone, anyone.'
Some people hard, that not right.
Me, I'm easy, I know, I know that one, I'm easy.

Give story little bit to other people.
Spread him out word.
And other people they might like him.

Your feeling, that's the trouble, your feeling.
Your body feeling, you make him easy, loose.
Work it out everything, with your blood or body, leg, arm.

You can't be hard, it's no good.
If you hard, something be happen to you.
I mean, I reckon meself, all these young, hard.
I know meself, hard that one now they getting.
Because something wrong heart.
Something wrong all that piece.

Heart attack, me.
I never get him heart attack.
I'm old man.
I should be go, but working more, more, more.

White people, they said, 'No more yet?'

I said, 'No, too much short wind, made me no good.
If wind should be good, I would work still yet.'

But that's wrong, I tell them.
Too much short wind, I don't like him.
So, I'm sitting in a wheelchair.
No good.

When you grow up now, see country.
You grown, no more young.
You don't get him young, you might go middle age.
You can look, he come to you, that feeling.
You get it, he hit your body.
You sit down, same now, same, and think about.
What I done, and all this.
What I done.

Even if wrong, it not too late.
More better you think about now.
You'll be good.
If too late, you can't do.
Aborigine people, I'm telling you earlier, you think about.
Do something, with your feeling.
With your body feeling.
Might be story.

If not, you can't do anything?
Can't think about any?
Climb rock, lookout like Ubirr, plenty stone here.
Climb top and sit down.

Look what kind, country what he saying?
He'll tell you country, there now top.
That other rock you can look.
He'll tell you what story.
Some spirit there, another rock.
You sit down, middle age, you say, 'Oh, I was wrong.'

Me, I been do.
That way I'm telling you.
Telling everybody now.
I been wrong.
Too strong me, and too hurry.

## OLD MAN'S STORY

I been argue uncle, old man, last one.
'Uncle?'

'Yes,'

'Ah, no matter,'

'Go on...'
This was argument, big argument.

'I got to go Darwin.'

'What for Darwin?'

'Well, good place, good country.'

'Your country, Ubirr, he singing out for you.'

I went and worked, work anything.
First, with white people, European, Darwin.
I went in there, make a friend.
I never drink then.
They showed me. I said, 'No, I don't drink.'

And feeling, I been very shamed.
Think about right back here.
I been sit down, think about here as little boy.
I been sit down, think about here.
'I can't go back, I won't go back,
I'm too far away, here in Darwin.'

I been come Croker, working there Cobourg, Black Point.
I been work there four year.
When I been getting middle age, early in the morning,
I was sitting down quiet, I nearly cry.

My uncle, he said, 'Yes, I know what you doing.'

'Yes,' I said, 'I think about.'

He told me, 'Don't think about, I know what you did.
So, that's it, I was telling you.'

I said, 'Yes, true.'

He open up your body, and that feeling, he come.
Might be good friend, you might tell him anything, what you was doing.
And I been come back alright.
They true alright, that old people, I growl them.

'No good you growl us, that your own fault.'

I been come back here now.
Forget Darwin.

Well, every people do that.
European he asking what Aborigine was doing before.
All that, same story, you want to know.
White people, I seen it, Sydney.
Ooh! true alright.
You can't work it out anyone.

I said, 'Ah, this European country now, walking along a street, we get lost.'

Same way, white man, here.
He get lost.
Same, all same.

## Law

I been little boy.

'It's time for you,' they been telling me.

'What time for me?'

They been throw bamboo spear, woomera.
'You make him shovel-nosed spear.'

'I can't make him,' I said.

'Time for you,' they told me.

## OLD MAN'S STORY

'This time not easy.
You got to do it.
Telling other people your feeling.
And this other thing: meaning, meaning of you.
What you think.

'What you think about, anything?
This thing you won't forget.
You'll forget, but he'll come back to you.
The meaning of your body, you'll be remember.
He open your body little bit, and you'll remember.
And you tell another man something.
That's the meaning.

'All this is Business.
I show you all sort of a thing, when you grow.
I show you, finish.'

They put line up, front of you.
Snake.
First time they been telling me, king brown.

'Grab it!'
I been frightened, no more little bit.

'Grab him!'

I was got to grab him that snake there.
Disappeared, like magic!
We see white man magic alright, Aborigine don't forget.
Aborigine magic too.
Too smart, blackfella.

All this going to be behind.
That mob now, they planned him.
When you go business, they'll show you.
Me, they been trick, snake.

Snake now, king brown!
'Grab him now!'

Uncle, he been there, front.
'Come on!'

He been head man, that business.
'You grab him!'

I bend down to get him, nothing there.
Uncle, he gone!

'Uncle, where you gone?'

'I'm standing here, back,' he said, 'behind you.'

'And snake, where?'

'Ah, you can't find him.'

That magic.
We don't tell anybody.

Unless you go look, yourself.

Crocodile!
'You jump, grab him!'

Crocodile big one!
You jump, you grab him —
Gone!
Crocodile, I don't know where he go!
Magic, that one.

These blackfellas, we say white man magic, haha!
Blackfella's the worse one.
Trick you.

. . . . . . . . . . . . . . . . . . . .

## OLD MAN'S STORY

That way from kid.
You got to grow, grow, grow.
They'll give you that all that story.
You can open up your body.
All these tree got name.
They'll give you all that.
And you'll do it after, yourself.

That way they told me, 'You won't see us.'
I don't see anybody.

'Ah,' I said, 'I'll see my mother.'

My mother, she said, 'No, you won't see me.'

'Oh.'

I think about now.
All gone.

This one for young, young.
I don't know what got to be.
They should listen, this one now, listen.
All the time, make him story, listen.
Put him tape, listen, and you get him.
But nothing, they walk away.

Leave him thing, white man.
White man stuff, leave him first.
After.
That for white man, we different way.

But nothing, they go their way, no good.
Because they don't know this one story I'm talking about.

European, he want more story.
So much white man he ask.
More better give it to him, story.
He'll know.
He might write him down.
He make him big one that book.
'Hey,' they say, 'where from, this one?'

'Ah, so and so.'

We got no anything.
More better we keep it story white man.
He got thing.
Pictures, story.
So we got story.

But white man, they go different way.
Different school, white man, and they don't know.
City, big city, that many people.
They don't know each other.
This feeling, and stories.

I been talking to one man.

Same thing, he said, 'We don't know.'

Well, all that story now.

## *Earth, our mother*

All this tree, grass, he watching us, he work with us.

Lot of story out of that tree.
I know only English is meaning.
Bit more that; your feeling.
Feeling.

You might say, 'That tree, same as young lady, or man.
Smooth, straight, looking good, you know, young.'

Tree, same thing.
You look tree, burnt one.
You mightn't like him, little bit.

But smooth, straight tree he grow.
That mean that tree, when it go dark, that plant, he grow slow in the night.
He grow, grow.

## OLD MAN'S STORY

That way he look smooth tree, and long.

And no fork, anything, all that.
Grass, he grow alright.
But he split all over the place.
If you want you can burn him.

Plain, billabong.
Plain you might walk.

You don't know what under that mud.

Aborigine, man or woman, he can find him turtle.

He know what there, he might dig up, and pick him up.
He can look when he swimming, or dry place he can look.
But when he buried, that long-necked turtle he stay next Wet.
When rain come he out, he start swimming.

Same all these.
Frog same.
Lizard, same thing, all that.
But we don't spread out what we had.
We had old people to tell us to look after.
Tree, grass, and world, this country.
Country, well look after.

Rock, don't worry about.
Might be cave, so you can live.
But rock, he won't help you.
He'll be there million, million year.

But we, we'll be going.
Rock he'll stay, we leave behind.
He can stay because he can't do anything.

But tree, sometime, sometime strong wind, he might knock him down tree.
All that tree and all these bushes.

Bandicoot, porcupine, snake, goanna, they grow later.
Sometime in the shade of all these small tree.
They live on the ground, some of them, some of them cave.

Possum, he climb.
He can see flower top, that ringtail possum he eat that.
He come down in the night.
He tell you that.
He don't feel it, I don't feel it.
I don't see him, he don't see me.

But he's there, with you, always.

You can see why he grow.
He growing, grass growing too.
When Wet come, little bit of wet, he grow.
Some grass, he grow dry country.
High country, tree same.
He grow.
He never tell that, but he doing it.

The meaning of that, meaning our mother, earth.
He doing it all that night, to grow that grass.

We don't know, nobody know, but he's there alright.
He look after us, one side.
He look after things.

We can't go just lay, sleep, forget about.
You forget about, sleep, he helping you.

But if you forget.
Forget and sleep, what you going to think about?
Think about, yourself.

You remember earth.
Our mother.

OLD MAN'S STORY

## *Caring, all the time*

Tree.
Like one tree, he split out.
Same as we.
A man each.

First, your mother.
This earth now, your mother first.
Now uncle, and father, that's the one they make you grow.
And telling you all this story.

They might say, father or mother.
'No, don't chop him down that tree.'
Because they knew, leave him.

Each Aborigine, we should live together.
Live together alright.
Stay together.
But should be this word, caring all the time.
Making story for children, for anybody.
Read it, tell you how.

Billabong, swamp, plain, river, that separate story.
Because he got crocodile, shark, in the sea.
Shark, might be one day he might come in, and kill somebody.
That's the one you'll be afraid.

Crocodile made before.
Crocodile Dreaming, to kill people, he promise.
There's one story, this he go.
Two sisters, crocodiles.
That Ubirr story, that story.

The bigger sister, she said, 'We won't kill woman, lady.'
And small sister, she said, 'No, we got to kill them, too.
Brother, cousin, uncle, we'll kill them all lot.
Even snake, king brown.'
That way we afraid, we got story.
They told us to explain to you.
Watch out snake, crocodile, shark.
All them dangerous.

That Aborigine people, all people what been dream here, they got that word.
They teach me.
They was teaching me every night.

'Now tree, he grow leaf, when he get strong, he grow leaf.
What that leaf?
He eating something, that tree.
If strong, we eat, we, we're full.
Till lunch, morning.

'That mean he eat something, that tree, from the ground, and make flower.
He's full.
He make flower for anybody, bird.
Some fruit he give us, plum.'

We don't live on now much, but children few.
I live on bush plants, plum.
Other people they forget that.
They give me heart like no good, feeling of me.

'You don't eat,' I say, 'you don't eat, why?'
Well, you know, they should eat too.
Kid, they like it.

We say, 'You got to eat.'
I been eating first, they teach me.
'You got to eat your fruit, he got flavour.'
Everything got flavour.

## OLD MAN'S STORY

Because, Dreamtime, man been living with the fruit growing in the ground.
This little boy, he might get him, because all the time I teach.
But teaching, he listen quiet.

But you might read it in a book.
The old tree, our grandfather, or grandad or auntie.
Young, young boy we say, young tree, baby.
That's the one he grow plants.
Might be little boy, little girl.
Same thing, all this.
He grow same way, growing with us.
We must think about all this, because they helping us.

But some people they don't worry about that.
That's bad.
You keep him, earth, well look after.
Some people don't like him, no matter.

Earth, he might do little bit good.
Sometime you might look yourself.
And you might say, 'Ah, what happen over there?'
You feel it yourself, he lovely, lovely country.
Well, in your word, he follow.

This one now, earth, world, sky.
What this sky for?
Blue sky, we say lovely, what that for?
Not himself, he might be working too.
Working with us.

## *Moon*

What about star, nice clear star, what that one?
What's that star?
He got Dreaming there, talking to us.

We can look moon.
But sometime, full moon, big moon, you look.
He get bigger, bright.
Have a look.
Look slow, what there?
What I tell you, I tell you.

You can look man with a spear, woomera, and dog.
And firestick and feather, of might be goose, to make fire.
You look slow, might be good for you.
You might understand, I don't know.
When you see full moon, he get bigger.
Slow you look.

What moon doing?
He give you this down here.
Earth.
What you see, he bright, yes, he bright.
What you can see?
Tree, something animal.
You can see man walking up.
White people, they got torch.
We, moonlight.

But moonlight, he come after, moon coming out.
And he start brighter, give you bright, to look something.
You know moon, he's the man.

## OLD MAN'S STORY

He give you bright, that man him along moon.
That's the man, Nadambarnee his name.
You can look man, woomera, spear, dog, goosewing and firestick.
He's there; I used to look before, good eye.

I said, 'Man along moon!'

'Yes, well that's the one, moon man there,' they used to tell me.
So, you can look.
I don't know about city, might be you can look easy.
White people you can look because you got glass, eh?
You can look closer.
You can make him, and you look, man there, dog.

And that man, moon, he went hunting.
That way he got goosewing, firestick, no matches, no lighter.
Now we got lighter, firestick Aborigine.
He gone hunting, made fire, cook might be goanna.
And he stand, he said, 'Where I got to go? Go back down earth?'
He sit down, think, think hard.
Only one way he was thinking,
'What I want to do?'

And dog, he come alongside.
'No, we stay up here.'
So him there along moon.

'We had enough hunting.
I don't want to go down there.
I go top; I stay moon.'

He stayed there.
'And you mob, you people here now, you can see me if you want.'

. . . . . . . . . . . . . . . . . . . .

Now, this feeling.
I say feeling, because feeling, everything what I'm saying is feeling.
He spread out, eh?
Somebody else feeling, somebody else feeling.
They should be one, feeling together, and talk about it.
That way, sometime, somebody sick, they miss that feeling.
If they keep him and teach children, might be good.

This part, this story, they teach me myself, and they said:
'Ah, you can keep him; split him out like word.'
Feeling, he got plenty story, word.
Only English, he beat me.
My word alright lingo, that way I'm doing half-half.
Feeling, and story, memory.
You think about little bit, eh?

Sit down, from tree.
You look tree, alright.
You think about your feeling.
What you want to do?
You got to help that tree, or what?
Are you going to talk about that tree?
Because he talk about us.
Watching us, what you doing.

Even grass.
Grass, wallaby he got to eat, eh?
He growing, he must grow.

This very hard.
Get this mob people to understand.
They won't understand.
Woman, old lady, they should be think about that.

## OLD MAN'S STORY

Only my mother, auntie, uncle and grandma.
They was knowed all these story.
Now, this mob here, this time, good woman, you can see.
But they don't know that story.
Nothing.

Wind, this one now, he blow, because I'm talking.
I'm talking, and he give you that wind.

Wind, he got medicine for your body.
He go through your body.
That our cousin, uncle, mother of this.
He sing out, what we do?

We don't know what he saying.
But you got to get there.
Anybody want to get there too.
No matter who you are.
But same story this.
We all go there.

One place, this earth.
Our mother.
And this earth, we came from there.

Before mother carrying, this important.
You feel yourself, just like little frog or something.
That we, he grow.

You grow, you grow.
She feel now, she carrying.
You know that?
If you know, explain to your wife.
Your wife asking question, she give you answer.

Love one another, that top, is nothing.
That love, another, that for white people.
We, another word, you know, another word.
That word, he good one.
Important, all that.

White European, he ask you.
He want story, so much story you got, he want to know.

In the night, he write him out.
Little tape you talk, speak, still write him book.
Good for him.
But you won't give it, that story.
You got to be careful.

Look after one another.
Look after country.
All this what I said, tree, grass, billabong, water.
You got to look after.
Not only one, but everybody.

But if you look after, and think about this.
Everyone, seem to me, all these things I'm talking about, all been forget.
Nobody using it.

But anyway, I just make this one here.
Make this one story.
Might be somebody keep this word.
Might be spread out little bit more.
Friend and friend.
They might like him.
Couple of book there, old generation they say.
Your feeling.

Sun, sunset, you can look sunset.
Good for you, I know you like it.
Sun, he say, 'Here, goodbye, I got to go.'
So he go red, little bit, down.
Sun is no good, he kill you.
Too hot, sun.
Moon, he good one.

Sun little bit dangerous.
He burn you.
We get up morning cool.
Soon as you get ten, eleven, might be lunch, close up, hot that sun.

## OLD MAN'S STORY

Because he done before us, and he done all the time.
They reckon he get hot, he get bigger.
And we get hot.
Cold weather, sun he go smaller.
And we feel him cold.

Wind, he got to blow.
Nobody can stop it.
He got special medicine for you:
'Ah, good wind,' we say.

Even water.
Water, rain, he come down.
He got medicine.
That way we drinking water.
Always water, to make you good, no water, we finish.

Water, medicine, good for you.
You can't go without water.
Everybody have water.

In this bush, ice water now.
White man came here, and make ice water.

Not us, you keep your story.
Just ordinary you can drink.
Too hot, or little bit warm, he's alright.
But if you go spring, cold water, running water.

You can't make ice.
Ice we don't know, Aborigine people we can't.
White men make ice, they got machine.
We, we can drink anywhere.

I'm drinking anywhere, because I'm used to it.
If I drink ice water, I'll be looking for ice water, ice water.
More better I follow my way.

Nobody do that.
Because no-one been tell you that, Aborigine people.
Plenty Aborigine people, but they never explain to you.

That why I'm putting this, little bit of story this.
Might be you people can listen.
Might be good one, might be bad.
I don't care.

Long as that story there.
Because he's good for you.
You can listen story, and good.
Good in the night.

## *Story good for you*

Animal.
He talking to us, that animal, bird.
White cockatoo.
That's the one they put Dreamtime to watch out.
If somebody come, he sing out from top.
That old people story, they used to say listen that.
And that true.

My grandfather: 'You listen, white cockatoo.
Somebody coming?'

I said, 'No, nothing, nobody.'

But uncle was walking there.
Next minute I look, uncle walking.

'Yeah,' I said, 'uncle.'

'What, that cockatoo tell you somebody coming?'
Many times.
I'm telling you, some of you boys, to get this story.
He good for you.

## OLD MAN'S STORY

You know what happening now.
Youngfellas they get sick, because no power left.
You got to hold this story, if you want to.
And story help you out.

Tree important, tree, grass.
Rock, he can't move.
He can't tell you, rock.
Him just sit down quiet.

But that painting, they put it there.
You will remember something.
You might dream, all that painting here.
Come and sit down.
And look, what happen this?
What they draw there?

Because these paintings behind children when they grow up.
Behind our children, that work they done.
Now, keep it, look after.
All that painting they done, no history book, no, only paintings.
All these paintings longa cave.
Important.
It's your story.
Good for you.
Good for me.

My story, I just put through your feeling, through your body.
Sit down and think about.
Which one you pick him up?
Which one good one?
You must pick him up good meaning of story.
Might be knowledge.
He work too.
Your body, yourself.

What blood doing?
You chop him that tree.
He got blood too.
You might say this water.
That blood, like you got blood.
Same thing.

Everything all same.
Same story.

School?
School might be good thing to learn.
But, might be now you mightn't like him.
Because lot of argument.

You can work office.
You can work everywhere, to make money.
The money important, causing lot of trouble.
You got to get little bit money, you got to go drink.
All that.
Why don't you keep up?
Forget that.

Money.
Might be money you fighting over, sister, brother.
Money for white European.
White European causing all the argument might be.
Argument from money, lot of trouble.

But story, lot of argument, can't be work.
You got to go back, listen to it, this story.
And talk about, and sit down, think.
If not, you can climb on top rock, moonlight.
And sit down, think.
Keep story all the children.
You can lie down moonlight, and tell your child story.
And little child can look star, he can look moon.
Might be he good sleep, he might dream.

OLD MAN'S STORY

My mother used to do for me, and grannie.
That way I got little bit story here.
Some of them I forget.
I went away, you see.
But anyway, a few of these paintings, give you feeling good.

Moon.
Sun is more bright.
Moon very fine, and cold, and bright.
He give you good sleep.

You can look up seven spirits.
They helping all that sister.
Crocodile up there, you don't know that.
Nobody know.
Snake, king brown eye, he's there, top.
They showed me everything.

I bet you sit down there, you go sleep.
I used to do like that.
That story make you sleep, and moon.
And seven spirits, all that.

This one now, where we sitting now, here we sit on earth.
Only one earth.
But this story should be spread out.
For anybody.

. . . . . . . . . . . . . . . . . . . .

# OLD MAN'S PICTURE

The Wet Season was advancing upon us fast, and with a sense of dread I would watch the storms darken the afternoon sky, lightning stabbing through the trees, rain falling for an hour or so. Then the evening announced itself with a spell of steamy sunshine, a chorus of frogs and chattering creeks, waterfalls cascading off the rocks.

But I was a worried man, for I wondered how the track to Chicken Hawk might have fared after the rain. Might it be too soft?

There was no point waiting until the next moonrise to take the picture; for, after all this rain, the track out there might be impassable. I finally decided that I would have to bring the shoot forward, forget the full moon and just shoot Old Man and Ricky together by the fire in the evening light.

I checked with Old Man to see what he thought.

'Yer, you go look. Take that top road, he more better, might be,' he said, fanning himself with a goosewing.

Old Man was right, the top road that went through Cannon Hill was the way to go. We could avoid the treacherous black-soil floodplain, and stay on sand which would stay firmer longer. The spot where I wanted to shoot was looking fine, the ground firm, the waterlilies in the billabong rattling in the breeze. A solitary crocodile watched me from beyond the leaves with just his eyes and snout above the waterline. He sank as soon as I saw him. I collected firewood in readiness for shooting the picture; there was no way I was going to miss this last opportunity.

I reported back to Bill, and all was arranged for Sunday night. I was working at Ubirr that night, but Darrin said he would cover for me, no worries. He was adamant that I had to get this picture, it was really important, and that I should not delay. The approaching Wet Season would play havoc with Old Man's fragile health; a bad bout of flu could spirit him away at any time, and there was absolutely no point hoping to delay the picture until the next Dry Season; Old Man might be gone by then.

So the fateful day dawned, the last day of October, and it was a beauty, clear and bright, not too hot, the country looking so good after the recent rain. Everything was arranged. Old Man was fine, and Ricky was at home.

At four, Darrin came bounding up to me.

'Off you go mate, don't delay! Good luck!'

I rushed back and changed out of my uniform, loaded up the truck with all the necessary gear and made it round to Old Man's house in good time. He was sitting there all alone. There was nobody else in the house, and no sign of Ricky anywhere. Old Man shook his head sadly, and said, 'Ricky he gone Oenpelli, cross the river. Family gone, everybody gone.'

I couldn't believe it, I just stood there dumbfounded.

I said, 'Let's go Cannon Hill, find another kid.'

## OLD MAN'S STORY

Old Man wheeled his chair towards the truck, he was anxious to get going. We hurtled towards Cannon Hill. How many times had we done this? It was like being caught in some dreadful time warp; a recurring nightmare.

We rolled into Cannon Hill but there were no small kids around, only Mick. He was twelve and already a strapping youngster; still, at this age he would be old enough to be under the guidance of an elder preparing him to go through Law, so a picture of them together would not be inappropriate. I asked Mick if he could help us out and he grinned and climbed right in.

We tore along the track to the billabong where the firewood lay stacked ready to burn. Mick got a fire burning, and together we helped Old Man from the cab, gently setting him down upon the ground below the gaunt pandanus trees.

I brought the truck up, hooked the generator to the battery, and set the flashlight just out of frame. The distant horizon remained clear, it was a beautiful evening.

I sat Mick down next to Old Man, but as he was almost the same size as Bill, there wasn't the impression of an elder passing on his knowledge to a child — the shot just looked like two Aboriginal men having a chat.

What to do?

My mind was made up. This was the way it was meant to be, all along: I would shoot Old Man on his own, looking to camera as if he was talking to us; the people looking at the picture. We were the youngfellas, all of us here on this little planet, and it was up to us now to look after the place, as his mob had done for so long.

I told Mick I would shoot Old Man on his own beside the fire. We moved him closer to the glowing coals. My window of opportunity, when it was light enough to see the country, but dark enough for the flames of the fire to be burning bright, was now only a couple of minutes. The light was dying. The sun had left the scene. It would be dark very soon. The flash flickered, shortly it would overheat and close down; I might get ten frames, no more.

My heart was beating fast, it was now or never. This was it, no more chances.

I left the camera, sat down in front of Bill, and said, 'Old Man, I want you to look in that lens as if you saying to that person who is looking at this picture, "Now YOU, you look after this story".'

I returned to the camera, told him I was ready, and to keep as still as possible.

I counted him down, one, two, three…

He lowered his head, and in the yellow glow of the light I could see his old eyes glowering right into the lens, like the coals in the fire. He was still as a rock.

This, at last, was the moment we had both been working for.

I pressed the trigger, the flash fired, and I can still see those eyes. Even now. His old shoulders slumped. He had put all of himself into that picture.

I shot a few more frames, but there was little point; the shot was in the can. We were done.

> 'My old people all dead.
> We only few left, not many.
> We getting too old…
> Young people, I don't know if they can hang on to this story.
> But now you know this story.
> Might be you can hang on to this story, this earth.'

The dark of evening descended upon us like a cloak.

In the soft glow of twilight I packed up the gear, the fire now nothing but a bed of coals beside which Old Man sat quietly as I loaded the truck. It struck me then that of all the innumerable fires that he had sat beside out here on the floodplain, this might be his very last. I moved slowly and respectfully so as not to disturb his thoughts while he stared into the glowing embers, and when Mick and I had carefully lifted him back into the truck I resisted the impulse to stamp out the last fitful glow of the ashes, and let the night gently take them instead.

We took Mick back to his house. I pressed one of my favourite harmonicas into his hand, just to say thanks, and he stood by the steps to his house and watched us drive away into the gloom.

I drove back to Old Man's house in silence. I was utterly spent, and I know that he was too. He had put all that he felt in those last frames, and it seemed to me that all our previous attempts had been leading up to that final conclusion. The picture spoke its truth between Old Man and the unknown thousands who would look at it one day, and see those old eyes looking right back at them, as if to say: 'Now you, you look after this story. You look after this earth.'

Just as he and the generations before him had done for all those countless years.

After we reached the house and I had turned off the engine, I said, 'I think we got good picture then, Old Man.'

'Good one, good,' he muttered, and then turned to me, and said, 'after this we finish, eh? All this take too much out of me.'

I nodded in complete agreement. I knew exactly what he meant.

# THE WET SEASON

The rains came nightly now, and I would lie on my swag in the back of the truck with the roar of heavy raindrops upon the roof, lightning flashing purple through the windows, thunder crashing through the trees, and I knew that my time here at Ubirr was drawing to a close. Soon this little settlement would be cut off from the outside world. During the next four months of the year this whole area would be inaccessible because the road to Jabiru (the only way out) would disappear under two metres of water as Magela Creek flooded, swollen by the rains cascading off the stone country. After that, the only way in and out of here would be by boat.

The Rangers would remain and look after the place; anyone else would have to leave East Alligator long before the waters were too deep to cross. This was a fact that gave Old Man some comfort, for his country would 'get some rest' from all the thousands of visitors who came yearly to Kakadu. However, he would also have to leave here, for his health was so fragile that it was necessary to keep him in Jabiru, close to the Clinic and the nearby airfield, just in case his health should take a sudden dive for the worst and the medics deemed it necessary to fly him into Darwin hospital; a scare which had happened a few times already.

Soon my job looking after the art sites at Ubirr would finish, and so I relished those last days as I paced the place on my rounds, absorbing the subtle changes in the vegetation and the lush green world which was now emerging, as if from sleep, after the early rains. I had got to know the place so well, and it saddened me to contemplate leaving there, so I drank in the sights each day: the little group of rock wallabies that lived under a rock shelter who would peer at me, still as stones, as I passed; the tawny frogmouth who stared motionless from the branches of a tree high above the path; the acrobatics of the iridescent rainbow bee-eaters as they swooped from their perches to catch an insect on the wing; the screeching evening chorus of black cockatoos as they lazily flapped past the lookout on their way back to roost for the night in the distant treetops. Each evening I would watch the sun sink as a golden disc into the billabong which was growing with each fall of rain, as honking mobs of magpie geese grazed around the edges. I had really come to love the place.

However, events were changing around me.

The Surveillance Contract had gone out for tender and Trevor had put in a quote, but he was informed it was too high and that he would not be needed next year. Someone else would look after Ubirr. So when his contract expired

I would be out of a job, Jamie too. There would be no money coming in and I would have to find somewhere else to live.

I still had work to do; for I had to transcribe all the tapes that I had made with Old Man to make sure that there were no mistakes. So I would have to move to Jabiru and find a place there to stay, as cheap as possible.

Meanwhile, the proofs of all the pictures had arrived.

I was happy with the shots of Old Man by the fire and I took them round to show them to him. My heart was in my mouth, for if he didn't like them then I really had a problem, for neither of us could go through that ordeal again.

'Mmmm, good one, yer, gooood,' he muttered, as he pored over the contact sheets.

I breathed a huge sigh of relief. The saga was over at last.

It was decided that Old Man's community would pay for the production of a printed poster of Old Man, and sell it to the tourists through the Marrawaddi Gallery at the Kakadu National Park Headquarters.

Trevor had been a printer before he had become a Ranger, and both of his brothers worked as platemakers in a Melbourne print shop. One of them, Dave, had worked previously in Kakadu doing surveillance with Trevor at Ubirr, and he knew Old Man well; they were firm friends. Dave insisted that he would print the poster, so I decided that I would trade in some frequent-flyer points and fly to Melbourne to get the job started.

I had one last day at Ubirr, and before I left I slipped round to the cave where Old Man had told his stories and thanked the spirits that lived there for their help, as water drops fell softly from the ceiling, and thunder rumbled, like Old Man's voice, through the trees.

I went round to see him, to say goodbye. I would be gone for a while.

Did he want me to bring him back something from the big smoke?

He looked around at his own vast array of personal possessions: a pair of shorts, glasses, wheelchair.

'Hmmm,' he scratched his head, and then his face lit up.

'Pipe, might be, yer, good one, and tobacco, please.'

I thought to myself that he really shouldn't be smoking, but on reflection, after a lifetime of tobacco, the damage was already done.

'Alright Old Man, I bring you a new pipe, and some tobacco too, alright?'

He nodded, grinning, three teeth in his head.

'Good one, thank you, friend. See you in Jabiru. Come see me when you get back.'

'Yup, boh boh, Old Man.'

'Boh boh, see you, friend.'

I shook his hand and walked away.

We were a subdued group of friends in the Training Camp that night, and I was grateful to all of them for their company over the last months. This was our last night together, our little band of stray dogs, and we'd all helped each other through this curious time together. Kate was off home to Geelong, and Trevor would soon fly to join his girlfriend in London. Darrin would stay here and work the Wet Season, and Jamie would look after Ubirr while I was away, but after the contract expired at the end of the month, he'd be leaving too. When I came back from Melbourne, I would be all on my own. Each of them had helped me while I was here and I knew that I would really miss their company.

Days later, I thought on all this as I looked out of the aircraft windows, the wide brown land slipping away beneath the wings. And that night, sleeping in my swag on a mate's floor in Melbourne, instead of the barking owls and the dingo howls, the night sounds were of sirens and the ringing of tram bells.

\*\*\*

Two weeks later I flew back to Darwin with the proof of Old Man's picture on board and drove back to Jabiru where I would now spend the next few months. Old Man was living there too, for he had been moved from East Alligator while I was away.

I went to visit him as soon as I returned, to show him the proof and give him his new pipe. He was happy with the picture and even happier with the pipe, but he hated living in town. Instead of living in an open dwelling out there in his own country he was now a prisoner of suburbia; stuck in a brick house with the rest of the family in a state of almost perpetual bedlam. His only possible escape was to wheel himself out into the driveway, there to look upon the other brick houses with their sprinklers on lawns, washing on the line. The mineworkers would drive past in their shiny Landcruisers towing boats on trailers and pay him no heed at all — they were earning good money digging uranium out of the ground, why should they care? He was just some old Aboriginal bloke sitting in a wheelchair, passing the time of day doing nothing much at all.

I found shelter with a tour guide and a pilot who had a house provided to them by the company they worked for, and we secretly agreed that I could stay rent-free in their spare room as long as I did the cooking and kept the house clean. Neither of them enjoyed cooking, and, as they were out all day, it suited me just fine.

It was a weird town to find yourself living in. Jabiru was built by the uranium mine to house its workers, and they still made up the principal inhabitants, each in their separate brick house, small garden, lawn, driveway, carport, big dog lurking behind the fence. Within walking distance there was a supermarket, shopping centre, bank, courthouse and cop shop, library, community centre and school, and a swimming pool of Olympic dimensions around which the inhabitants of suburbia lay like pale worms beneath the planted palm trees.

Here also were the headquarters of Kakadu National Park, and nearby, hidden behind the trees, lived many of the Rangers in their own separate dwellings grouped around the Bowali Headquarters, only a few kilometres out of town.

One mob digging up the country, the other trying to look after it.

And the tourists visiting in their thousands every year in cars, buses, four-wheel drives and tour groups, camped together in the caravan park or at the only hotel. While the Aborigines, whose country it was, stayed out of town in their own camp, some working as miners, some as Rangers, some as tour guides, some not working at all.

Once a week, a convoy of trucks would leave the mine and rumble along the only road to Darwin, trailers loaded with containers full of uranium yellowcake, radioactive for thousands of years.

Indeed, a curious town to find yourself living in.

Even more so if you are a traditional owner and your people have looked after that country for thousands of years. Yet each day you sit outside in your wheelchair on a concrete driveway and watch the world go by, unheeded and unrecognised.

There was work to be done, for, as we had agreed, I had to write out every word that Old Man had recorded on tape so that I could read it back to him and make sure that there were no mistakes. Here I was lucky; for Jabiru had an Open Learning Centre where anyone could learn to master a computer. I was given a security card so that I could let myself in at any time and work away in air-conditioned comfort while the rain thundered down upon the roof. After a few hours my eyes would be shot from staring at the screen, and I would have to call it a day. I'd walk out of there and saunter up the steaming streets to the footy ground to watch sixty blokes chase two balls and kick them over four sets of goalposts, while two referees ran around the pitch, puffing into whistles.

Weeks later, I took the fifty pages of text around to Old Man who was sitting on his bed underneath a spinning fan. Around him, stretched out like corpses upon the floor, were several of the youngfellas who were still sleeping off the effects of a late night at the club. They remained quietly snoring while I sat on the bed beside Old Man, and began to read. He listened attentively, nodding in agreement whenever a sentence referred to his young people leaving the ways of the whitefella world and returning to their culture. One of the corpses stirred and sheepishly staggered out into the daylight after a particularly pointed reference to the youngfellas mending their ways.

I would read him maybe twenty pages at a time, for periods of peace and quiet were few and far between in that house, but after several visits we were finished. I was glad that for the later readings we were joined by members of his family, who sat closely beside me and listened in total silence while Old Man puffed away on his pipe, like a vision lost in smoke.

When I had finished the last page and the little audience had filtered out into the daylight, silence fell upon the room. Old Man put down his pipe, cleared his throat, and wheeled himself closer.

'Good one,' he said, 'you done good job.'

Then he placed his two palms together, as if in prayer.

'I reckon we been work like this,' he said, placing fingertip to fingertip, palm to palm.

*\*\**

A week later I came round to the house with a box of fruit. He was sitting outside in the shade. I peeled him a banana, and when he had finished it, he said, 'Might be we do some more story, eh?'

'Yes, sure, Old Man, when you want to do that?'

'Tomorrow might be good. He good for you?'

'Sure, Old Man, no worries. Might be storm in the afternoon, morning might be more better.'

'Yer, good one, thank you friend.'

When I returned it was a beautiful sunny morning. Clouds were passing fast overhead and a warm wind was worrying at the trees. The house was full of screaming kids so we drove around the town looking for a peaceful spot, eventually ending up at the footy ground. Here were some large shade trees where he liked to sit whenever he watched a game, so I spread a blanket on the damp grass for us to sit upon, and when all was ready, I gave him the nod.

## OLD MAN'S STORY

Fallen Tree, Nardab Floodplain.

Old people, they used to pass away.
Might be father or mother, auntie or cousin, used to stay there.
Get stringybark, make a bed.
They used to build a bunk in the bushes.
They used to say, 'Well, we better leave them here.'

They used to leave him, might be one year, and go back.
Take him back paperbark, and collect all that bone.
Bone and skeleton.
They used to cry, 'You got to go back.
Stay your cave, your own country.'

THE WET SEASON

Alright, they used to go home.
Make him ceremony now.
Paint themselves, arm, the Law, and have corroboree.
Say goodbye.

They used to go sleep, they hear that clapstick.
'Hey, he's there alright! He come back.'
And old people, they used to say, 'He's alright, leave him.
Leave him skeleton there.'

But this time like, they change.
And spirit, not much.
New generation, old people they dying.
All in a box, no good.

I mean we Aborigine, we should keep him our Law always.
That where something wrong.
We follow white man, something wrong.
Now, little bit wrong now.
We should be follow our Law.
Follow our custom.

And skeleton, keep him in a cave.
Spirit they should come back, talk to us.
They there.

My people, they come back their skeleton.
I never put him box.
They been come back, talking to me.
I seen it meself, and I believe.

You people, nothing, you don't believe nothing.
This European way is different.
We should keep our Law, skeleton, everything.
Take him back right place.

You mob follow European law.
We should keep him our Law.
And now we want to be teach together.
Might be good.
We teach one another.
And that people they should come out properly.

My uncle, he was last one.
He told me, 'Don't get that coffin box.
I don't want him.'

I said, 'What for?'

'No, I don't need, I won't come back.
You lock me up.'

I said, 'Yes, I believe you, what you saying.'

'Yes,' he told me, 'if you get box, I won't see my cave.
If you believe me, what you believing, white European?'

I said, 'No, not really, I believe you, what you say.'

So, old man, he said, 'Two week I got to leave you behind.'
Six o'clock morning he wake me up.
'You hear me?'

I said, 'Yes.'

'Come.'
I came close.

He said, 'I got two week.'

I said, 'Uncle, you make me sorry.'

'Don't sorry,' he said, 'you forget that.
You can just leave me, and skeleton.'

And close now, he said, 'Two day, I got to talk with you tonight.'
'Yes,' he said, 'this last one, my boy, this last one talking to you.
I'll be talk to you, I got two day.
Don't be sorry or think about.
She'll be right.'

Anyway, uncle been pass away two day.
Everybody been there.
I told boss I used to work.
'I got to go, because got to be funeral.'

'We should get him box.'

## OLD MAN'S STORY

I said, 'No, old man didn't like him, you got to follow our way.'

'Ah, alright,' he said.

Anyway, he gave me tucker, everything.
We had big ceremony there, after, tucker.
His daughter, everyone, we had good feed.
Morning we took old man, put him away.

Well, I said, 'Everyone, you listen to me.'

'Yes, go on.'

'You know river, or creek, running water?'

'Yes.'

'He run water, he run out spring, he cut off.
This old man, now he pass away, same thing he told me.
Now skeleton, if skeleton he stay box, that way uncle said:
"You lock me up, no good, I won't come back.
I like come back and talk to you."'

And he done alright, he come back alright, and true, I believe.
My uncle used to be buffalo shooter, and he gave me hard time.
If I go talk to old man, uncle, I won't be used that wheelchair again.
I'll be walking.

He come back soon, that way we say spirit.
I was laying down there, lunch, two o'clock, and old man he come.
'Get up,' he said.
'Wake.'

'Who you?'

'Just get up, look me.'

And, my friend, I been look that old man.
Youngfella, clean shave everything, black hair.
Him and my wife, they been come together.
This true, God.

And he told me, 'What I said, you didn't believe me, eh?'

I said, 'Yes, might be.'

'You didn't believe me what I said, and you look, your wife there.'
I see my wife, young girl this one, young.

'You can't come close,' he said.
'No, because something you been smoke yourself.
You should know.'

And that true.
Old man been come out, stand up, talking to me.
I was start to cry for him.

He said, 'Don't cry.
Come place.
Come over that place.
You come there.
You stay yourself, and I tell you what's going on.'

And he done it alright, old man, uncle.
He done good job.

I said, 'Ah, you done good job.'

'No, you, you done good job for me.
You been believe me.'

I said, 'Yes, I been believe you.
You was telling me story.
You made me sorry, sorry, and that's it.'

He said, 'Oh well, you can't be sorry again.
You look me, young.'

## OLD MAN'S STORY

And I said, 'I believe alright.'

'Come over that place now and wait for me.'

I said, 'Well, if I go there, I'll sing out, yell out.'

'You don't have to yell out, I'll watch you.
Just make him camp, make a fire, by yourself.
I'll come, we can stay together.
And I tell you everything what I got.
If you miss, no good.

'Good cave there,' he said.
'Your mother, your father, they there with me.
And three uncle, and grannie, all there, one place.'

That where that skeleton.

He told me, 'I'll come back again.
I'll see you, I'll come back.'

'But uncle, you young.'

He said, 'Yes, got to be young, that skeleton, leave him behind.
I get new, like clothes you change, get new clothes.'

That way your skeleton do that.
Lot of people don't know.
Balanda he don't know, he other way.

My wife she was sitting down.
'Your wife over there,' he said, 'talk to her.'

I said, 'Hello.'

She said, 'Hello.'

My wife, she been there, young girl.
I said, 'Come over close.'

But silly man me, I said, 'Hold me up.
Smoking, smoking, I sit down.'

'No. I get burned.'

I said, 'What for, you get burned?'

'You should know yourself.
What for you been grown up?
Smoke yourself, so I get burned?'

'I see.'

'You mad, right,' she been telling me, 'you mad.'

Ah, true, I been think about after, true alright.
I been spoiling meself.

'I want to come back and see you, sleep with you,' she said.
And that true, young girl.
How she been go young girl?

'Don't ask any question, I'm young, alright.
You come over, I'll come out with you.'

'How come?'

'Well, you been spoil him, yourself.
Well, you're wrong, true, you ought to leave them alone.
I want to come out, walk straight to you.
We want to camp, stay.
I want to tell you anything story.
And now, story, you got story, but wrong.'

I said, 'True.'
'But,' I said, 'you was longa coffin.'

'My father, he drag me out.
Well, I'm here, his daughter now.'

I said, 'I believe now.'

## OLD MAN'S STORY

He gave me how many years. He told me when I ready.

He said, 'When you wake up morning, you will see me.
Me and your wife, my daughter.
And we'll walk straight to you.
And world will be changed.

'I'm telling you now,' he said, 'but little bit wrong.
Other people, keep you down, you know.
You doing alright, but you should be free yourself.
But people giving different Law, Aborigine, eh.'

I said, 'True.'

'What about you, darling?' I said,
'What time you'll come out?'

'Might be one day, darling.
One day when my father ready.
You can see us walking.
And this world he'll turn.
You find him people, white people, good people.'

I said, 'Well, too hard.'

'World can fix him up, don't worry.'

'Well,' I said, 'me, I might be pass away, I'll see you.'

He said, 'You got long way to go, but I'll see you, I'll find you.'

'If I get sick, if I pass away, I'll be alongside you. We can start walk.'

'Haha, yes.'

I said, 'That's different story you telling me.'
My wife, I been look that young girl.
'Don't worry,' she said, 'I'm alright.
Well, we going now.'

Uncle said, 'We going now.
But, so and so place, you meet me there.
One place there, you wait for me.
I'll come out, talk to you.'

So I'll try, go.
Children they can go, make him camp.

I said, 'Well, I'll sing out for you. You can listen.'

'I'll be watching you, I'll be there.
I'll watch you make a camp, I'll come.'

'Why?' I said.

'Because when I was telling, you was believing me.'

'Alright.'

I been listen, he good.
They gone.

'You'll be alright!'

'Might be,' I said.

. . . . . . . . . . . . . . . . . . . .

Spirit is true, spirit.
For old people, they make me think.
Old people, you know, good people, solid.
Good people.
And spirit, they there.

This one here, not liar, all true.
Spirit, they there, man, like we.
They watching us, what we doing, they watching us.
And that's right too, yes, he's true that one.

## OLD MAN'S STORY

If liar, I didn't want to see.
I ought to tell liar, but I seen it my eye.
They been wake me up, and talking to me.
Uncle, he was talking to me, lingo, he told me everything.

That way, all these feelings now, I just give you all this.
What are skeleton.
I say skeleton belonga cave.
And skeleton we got to pick him up.
We'll go cave, put that skeleton there.
We go sleep someway, and he can listen corroboree.

You can listen clapstick, all that business now.
Spirits they here.
This man he talking, he good man, he know us, they say.

When I sleep, good sleep.
Good man, he talk about us, and we helping him.
Night, they help me.

I'll pass.
Look after.
It's true, all that.

And old people, they explained to me.
Ha! I used to say, might be liar.
But true alright, I been work it out meself, oh true.

Spirit, spirit can stand up rock.
If you sit down there, he with you, he look after you.
No matter where you go, he follow you.
'Hey,' he say, 'hey, wrong place you going.'
No matter how far, twenty mile.
Spirit he make you come back.

Not really spirit, but each people body.
People, they just listen to us, but we can't see them.
But they can see us alright, they can see us anytime.
No matter where we go, they watching.

Spirit, but really people, and that true, I believe meself.
Spirits, they watching us, no matter how we can say.
Now we talking spirit, they happy.
'They talk about us. That's good.'
They like him.

They might have big corroboree somewhere.
We can't listen, but they will.
That spirit is true.
One spirit is man, skeleton is nothing.

We can't worry, spirit is true, no matter how much we can say.
They stand behind us, talking to us.
But we can't listen.
Spirit people, they like him.
They help us, everything.
You say spirit is nothing.

You know nothing, it's true.

People don't understand.
They don't know what spirit, but they should know.
They think everything new, no good.
All the way, sit down, think about.
That's it, but no.

*Is there spirit in everything that lives, Old Man, spirit in tree, spirit in bird?*
Tree, he open them like door, one of these tree.

*Spirit in the moon up there?*
Moon, they there.

*We got spirit around us everywhere?*
Around everywhere, no matter where you go.
We can go, but they look after us.
Climb sunset, they there, spirit.

## OLD MAN'S STORY

Ubirr, they look after.
When you talking them there, they there.
They say, 'Ah this good man, this one.'
That way they happy.

But that way I said we been get mix-up European way.
We fallen wrong, we been going to keep it separate.
Aborigine separate.
Now, we ought to tell him story, really.
Now we ought to join one another, and talk over.
And he's true.
But now, got me beat, wrong.
We been wrong, Aborigine people.
Another mob they been spoil him us.
But spirit they there, but they slow down, I think.
Plenty Cannon Hill.
Spirit, my father might be there, mother.

Other people they don't listen, no good.
You might listen.
Listen, 'Alright, spirit, they there.'

Always, no matter where you go.
No matter where, they watching you.
Those spirits, this tree here, he can open him like door.
And he can stay there, with tree.
Easy.

Spirit, him here, spirit.
They sit down, listen.
These people they good, nice.
Well, good.

But plenty people I'm telling, Aborigine.
But they give me wrong, you know, wrong idea, feeling.
Wrong idea what I'm telling is true.

## THE WET SEASON

They don't listen, no matter, the spirit is true.
Spirit can help you.
You can sleep, way up you can sleep.
This true, I been try meself.
Like talking to you.

That way I'm talking to people.
I'm doing this one, skeleton and spirit.
And no more, it's true that.
They can't miss you, they can't miss you and me.
They always there with us.
We should follow our Law.

But these Aborigine people.
All them too much think about something else.
I think about that.
Because the spirit, the old people, old generation.
Generation to generation, that's that skeleton.
Must go back longa cave.

These people beside Ubirr.
They been do wrong too.
Skeleton, they never pick him up.
That way I'm saying, well, we been just box him up.
No good.

You ought to leave him balanda law.
Leave him outside, leave him out.
Balanda law after.

We been going to take him white man.
White European, take him here, over here.
He got to be here, on top.

## OLD MAN'S STORY

You know money business.
We want to get him money business.
I don't worry that money.
I think about other way.
I sleep good.

We Aborigine people, we been box him up one, balanda side.
We got to go another way.
Stay away, should be good.

Because, burial ground, burial ground you go sleep close.
He can listen.
I seen it everything myself, and I believe.

Yes, you can sleep yourself.
He come out, talk to you.
'Hello, friend, hello, how you?'

'I'm alright.'

You might answer them.
Or somebody might answer, and he's true.
Now we been box him up, no good.
Idea no good, me, I don't like.

Stay there, so you get big mob spirit, helping you.
But nothing, these people they forget about.
Wrong, that wrong.
You should be think about.

But no, you want to think about, alright.
Well, he should be.

Our people like moon.
And close up that story, no matter who skin.
But we been spoil one another.
We, Aborigine people, white people.
Too much fight, spoil.

But he'll come one.
This one now, this story now.
I just take him out because I never tell anybody, you know.

Well, might be good, I don't know.
But, he alright.
They'll be alright.
Spirit alright.

They winning us, spirit.

. . . . . . . . . . . . . . . . . . . .

Old Man remained quiet for a long time, sitting motionless on the blanket, and the expression upon his face was as if his mind was far away.

I turned off the tape and sat there quietly with him in the shade of the trees. I felt as if the old spirits that he had referred to were around us, silent witnesses to their story, and that they were happy that their tale had been told. Then he gave a little nod, as if answering a question from a voice that only he could hear, and looked up at me as if it was time for us to go.

When I had packed up and helped him back into the truck, he turned to me and said, 'What I talk about today, I never talk about before.'

He didn't speak again.

Only when I had left him at the house did he give me a little wave farewell, and quietly say, 'Boh boh.'

When I returned home, I made for my little room and closed the door. After what I had just heard from Old Man I didn't feel like talking with anybody. Outside my window the day darkened, the rain fell heavy on the roof and I lay upon my swag in the darkness with Old Man's voice still in my head. Hearing him talk about his wife made me want to ask him more about her; for I knew that he had only one wife, all of his life. She had died some years ago, and he had never looked at another woman. He must have loved her very much.

Should I ask him more about her?

***

OLD MAN'S STORY

The morning sun came bounding in through the window, and I was out of bed and into the bush for an early walk. The grasses were sparkling, the trees still dripping, and showers of raindrops fell as busy birds leapt from branch to branch. It was a truly beautiful morning.

I bought some fruit and took it around to Old Man who was sitting outside in the early sun while the rest of the family slept.

'How you Old Man?' I asked, as I peeled him a banana.

'Goood. Good sleep,' he grinned, 'good dreams too.'

I was tempted to ask him about his wife, and whether he had been thinking about her in his dreams, but before I could summon the words, he said, 'More better we keep our dreams within us. Soon as we tell them, they fly away and fade from us.'

So I kept my questions to myself.

# THE LAST STORY

The Wet Season had been running late, but now the monsoon broke and the skies darkened as heavy rain fell upon us for hour after hour, day after day. The air was so humid that everything became clammy to the touch, damp clothes became mouldy, and it was tempting not to venture out at all.

I feared for Old Man's health; this was the weather that really knocked him about. His old lungs would be having a hard time dealing with the damp, so it came as no surprise when some of the family spotted me in the supermarket and told me that he was unwell and that things were not looking good.

I made him a concoction of hot ginger tea and went round to the house.

He was sitting slumped in his wheelchair beside the door to the garden, his head hanging low. I patted his knee, and he said, 'Hello', very quietly. He raised his head and said he wasn't feeling well. He looked terrible; his eyes were way back in his head. He asked me how they looked.

'Not good, Old Man,' was all that I could say.

I thought that I would leave him be so that there was no need for him to talk, I just poured a hot cup of ginger tea for him and left it close at hand.

He thanked me and said he'd feel better soon, might be.

'Just take it slow Old Man,' I said, patting him gently on a clammy shoulder.

Back out into the endless rain, I was worried for him. This was the time of year when he was most fragile, and it had been during previous Wet Seasons that it had been necessary to fly Old Man into Darwin when his health took a turn for the worst. He had little defence against the damp and a sudden dose of flu, or worse, pneumonia, could carry him off at any time, snuff out his life, like a candle in a storm. What if he should pass away now? Had he told all of his story, said all that he had wanted to say?

I was a nervous man, watching the weather from inside my clammy little room.

\*\*\*

## OLD MAN'S STORY

The monsoon trough moved on, and the skies cleared. The sun made a very welcome reappearance and my anxiety lifted, so I walked along the steaming streets to Old Man's house. The family greeted me outside with wide grins and told me the old fella was feeling better.

I crept inside the empty house, the TV was off for a change. He lay asleep upon his bed. I went over to his sleeping form and stroked his white-haired head.

'How you?' rumbled his voice.

'Fine, Old Man, I'm glad you're feeling better. I was worried. How you feel?'

'Better. Lil bit.'

I wished him well, and crept away.

I left him in peace for a few days so that he could get his strength back, but when I eventually put my head in the door he was sitting on his bed looking quite chirpy. His old life force had returned and it was very good to see. We greeted each other and he motioned for me to join him on the bed.

He said that he'd had a dream while he was sleeping, and that we were at Alamangere, the cave with the old spirits, he and I, and Ricky too, and that his uncle and his grandpa's spirits were there as well, and they were happy that we were talking about them.

'And Jamie, he there too.'

I knew that Old Man really missed Jamie.

'He like son,' he had said.

I had a mental picture of our little group sitting outside the cave as Old Man told his story with the shadowy forms of the old spirits watching over us, and thought to myself how precious this tale was, and what a responsibility I had to ensure that it was told.

'I was worried when you were sick Old Man that you might pass away before you had finished your story. So I thought I'd ask you, now you're more better, is there any more that you want to say?'

'Yer, might be,' he said, stroking his bristly chin.

'Well, you tell me when you want to do that, eh?'

'Right, yeh, I think about, ma, good one,' he nodded.

He took a sip of his cuppa tea.

'I have good sleep and think about.'

I got up to leave.

'Come see me tomorrow.'

\*\*\*

The clear silver light from a full moon shone through my window before the first glimmer of dawn. I lay in the moonbeams and thought of the old man up there with his dingo and his firestick, and wondered how long it would be before this Old Man was up there too, looking down upon us all. Then I was up and out of bed early into a clear and sunny day with just a layer of cloud upon the horizon. It almost felt as if the Wet Season was gone.

A good day for telling story.

I went round to Old Man's house and he was sitting calmly on his bed. He'd slept well and enjoyed the moonlight too. I wheeled him to the truck and helped him aboard with a distinct feeling that now was the last time we would be doing this. There was a strange sadness and beauty in the act of sitting him down in the shade of a big old tree so that he could tell his story for the last time. It seemed that we moved in slow motion, as in a dream.

I set up the microphone and sat quietly beside him until he was ready.

He took a drink of water, and then he said, 'Right.'

## OLD MAN'S STORY

Ubirr Trees in the evening light.

You know that our people, this time they spread out.
But you was kid, somebody else's kid.
That's your start.
They would have been start from kid.

I was keeping that, Ubirr, they teach me.
I was follow them, and they said, 'No, go back.'
And they teach me all that painting.

THE WET SEASON

But land, this one.
This is the best way you grow.
And see the world, country.

Some of these trees got name, all that.
Little piece, little piece.

## OLD MAN'S STORY

Ten, I went walking around for a while.
I was eleven, I come back school.
I went school Oenpelli, and I went away again.
I didn't like much, because, you know, too many people.
You don't get enough of what you want.

I did, I said I want to get him in, all this, so I'll keep him.
If I lose, bad luck for me.
But I done alright, I still keep this story.
And now I'm doing it this.

Will you think about, Aborigine people?
Read it story this, because going to be nothing left.
Read it another kid, another woman, another man got to be understand.
One road.

You got to understand all this.
The story for you, because you won't be seeing me much.
You can see photo, I'm talking now, picture.
But you got to keep your story.
Teaching your kids, what world for.

World for anybody, no matter who.
But you got to keep him.
Keep on teaching.
No matter school, no matter that.
University, you can go university, you still hang on.
It's your finger, it's your body.
Put it into your string, your memory, knowledge.
Everything got to be in.
And teach children.
Hard, hard like school.
But hard.
You got to be teach hard.
So he can keep him.

Might be university, school, but this is the one.
It's good for you, good for anybody, to understand something.
One world, you got to understand that.
You can't be one man, myself.
The world everybody.

Don't miss.
If you mistake, you miss, that's the one something happen to you.
You must keep him, I'm telling.

Your body give up, but do this one better, and you'll come alright.
If you rush, you miss, is no good.
No good for anybody, he can't come back to you again.
Best to start with it, and keep going.
Still you go, you can go read it my book.

This the one, I giving you early.
Soon as you finish that book, you sit down and think about now.
Too many noise, get away.
Go some way and sit down yourself.
What I want to do, or what I want to teach?
You can pick him up easy, I done that.

They used to send me up the rock and sit down sunset.
Look open country, plain, and I used to ask question:
'What that billabong for?'
I mean swamp there, lily growing.

They used to say, 'That way lily, way you eating it now, now fruit.
And long-necked turtle he under that water, and file snake.
You want to forget all these things?'

I said, 'No, I'll try me best.'

'Alright.'

## OLD MAN'S STORY

Every afternoon I used to go back and look.
But now, I'm putting this one now book.
Will you read it?
Because you won't see me, might be sometime.

What coming to your body, and feeling and knowledge?
What you want to do?
You think about, very hard.
Don't miss out, because if you miss, you won't get much.
So you do it proper, good job for you.
You got child, you got wife.
Just matter your wife too, because the kids important.
And you find kids, when they grow bigger, they'll have good knowledge.
No matter school.

Because this country, here we sitting, he was no houses.
No, all this bush.
No house here, so we try teach you, putting this word.
So you want to understand, you might like him, might be not.
If you like better for you, I reckon.
Good for kid, good for your wife.
Anybody can do that.

You look rain, world.
Rain for us, no matter where you from.
You'll be remember, think about country.
He'll help you, the country, paintings, cave painting inside.

They took them inside, away from the rain, and they painted.
And they said, this got to be people to look.
So always people there, that your body, my body.
If you look, you want to take some word for you.
You can take him. You can write him down. You can take picture.
He won't hurt that, so you'll be remember, I suppose.

City; no matter you in city, sorry that.
You come from city, and quieter here.
You need this one more.

Do it, do it hard for you.
He go through your body.
What that mean, I mean your feeling, in your sweat.
Your feeling, he'll come to you.
Help you.

What this grass here?
All the grass, what makes that?
Rain, eh?
We all drink rain.

Rainwater, we'll drink water, grass help us, he drink too.
Tree, pandanus there, any kind tree, he help you.
Now he stop, he not help us.
And grass he don't grow, he stop.
In the night we go bed, we go sleep, he waking now.
Anything, star, moon, damn lot.

Star, moonlight, what that sign?
Sometime you look, moon he give us sign.
That's like you got torch.
He sign this world for you and me.
You and me.

You say, no, not mine.
It's yours alright.
When you go sleep, he working with you.
And old people, all been dead long time ago, they there.
They help you too.

Get all this, they say, get this.
Get this feeling for you, and kids.

Sometime kid he cry, he dream.
That good, he dream.
More better for him.
Because he'll be good kid.
I was doing like that.

OLD MAN'S STORY

And I'm not telling you a lie or something.
But he'll be a book.
All in a book.

Truth, in your feeling, he go through.
Feeling, your feeling, my feeling, somebody feeling.
You was looking for this.

This is story, but what your story?
For kids?
I'm telling you this.
It's time for you to think about.
It's not too hard.
Easy.
Think about, in your head, body.
What about you think about yourself, and get in this.
What you want to say?
Yes?
No?
I think yes is better.

No is too late.
No-one.
No-one can make that story.

## *Hunting*

Right, I start off that, young.
Night, I used to come back, laying down.
They teach me.
'You want this one, or you don't want it?'

I said, 'I'll try.'

'What! You want to try!
You'll have to keep him, long time.'

'But, what about you mob?'

They said, 'No, you won't see us.'

'What for?'

'The world, we can't save him ourself.
World and earth, we got to go earth.'

Alright, your grandpa, or mother, you got father, or some.
You know, they going.
Your father he's the one he can teach you.
Mother, she can listen to you.
Father and auntie, and uncle.
Uncle hard, too hard, he can teach you hard.
Auntie, I used to run away, I used to get belt.
Auntie used to give me hiding.
'Come back, sit down.'

But you know kids, I was kid.
You know when you get kids, little bit nuisance.
I used to nuisance, but Auntie used to belt me.
After that I give it away, getting hiding.

'This plain, what that plain for?
Plenty things there.
Plain, that plain for goose to lay egg.
That way he lay there egg all over the plain, water there.
We can't go and get him, but he lay egg.
Lily, he grow there, good fruit.
Better than yam, long yam, brown yam, cheeky yam.'

You never see that one now, because nobody getting it.
We people woman too lazy.
You should eat.
We get flu, everything.
You should clean up, clean him up body.
All that bush fruit.
But I always telling, just listen to me.
You want to get in this.

## OLD MAN'S STORY

Lily nuts.
You never see lily nuts, goanna, goose.
You can see goose, get, this day.
But before they was climbing tree.
They used to climb with couple of pieces stick.
They used to get him goose, because closer.
Too far when they fly, so they was up tree.
But nobody using it now, too much shotgun.
So goose they go other places.
I used to pick them up, Ubirr now.

I went Oenpelli school.
My grandpa, grannie, I was with them, all the time.

'Well, we got to leave you here, youngfella,' they told me.

Oh, made me no good, feel no good.

They been see me, they gone now.
They was walking up that plain.
I was school house, I come out, look, grandpa walking.
I said, 'I got to go!' and I was running.
They been look me, this one him now coming.
They been sit down, wait for me.

'What for! Why don't you stay with uncle and auntie?'

'No!'

'Alright, we go camp there. Rock.'

And my uncle, he come horses, auntie, she was walking up.
'You want to stay with me?'

'No.'

'No matter,' uncle said, 'he can go, but I'll be there, next week.'

Alright, we went there, we made camp.
I been happy now.

My grandpa said, 'Well, youngfella, what you want to do?'

'Nothing.'

'Can't be nothing!
You got to eat yet.'

'Alright; give me that spear.'

He gave me spear, wire for fish.
I went, I get two barra.
Grandpa, he been cook two.
One they been wrap with paperbark.
One we been eat.

I said, 'Well, what we got to eat morning?'

'Take him out that paperbark.'

I been on to him that paperbark, that meat was hot and good taste.
We been eat.
'Now, I'm tired of it, fish.
I go honey,' I said, 'I'll get him; give me axe.'

I been go now, I went, get honey, two billycan.
I come back, I was tired, no more hot, but sweat.
I got honey, give them.

That way now I got learning from hunting.
Get everything.
We don't get him now.
I used to get him file snake, that bugger, him been frightening me.
I been run like, ooh!

'What for you run away?'

I said, 'Snake!'

'Oh, that file snake, him alright.'

'But I got him on a spear!'

## OLD MAN'S STORY

Grandpa been come, get that spear, lift him up that file snake.
'He good eating, this one, don't stay away long way, we got to eat.'

So we roasted, cook.
He break him up, open him up.
Grandpa said, 'Come, taste.'

I been taste him.
Oh, lovely. Good one.
We been eat him.

Next time, long-necked turtle, we been swim, pick him up, turtle everywhere.
We been heave him up, roast him.
After cook, open him out, oh lovely!
We been eat.
Lily, we been eat, that's the first time.
Honey, we went up mountain, rock, walking up.

'Well, look! that big snake!'
He was laying down longa gully.
'Grandpa! snake, big one!'

'Ah, leave him,' he said, 'that snake too strong, he might tear you up.'

Alright, we go; they been sit down.
'Now, youngfella,' he said, 'you got to go in this jungle.'

'What for?'

'Just go in there, take him spear.'

I took spear, I went in jungle, look up tree, goanna everywhere.
I got four, I been come back, chuck him.
We roast him, proper fat one, that goanna.

Now we got to go beach for a while, see uncle, another uncle been there.
Alright, we been sit down.
Get turtle, big turtle from saltwater, we been eat.
And one old man, he died now, he made me friend.
I tell him, 'We go, friend. We been go beach now, get stingray, crab.'
We been come back, I been happy now.

That way hunting better for you, Aborigine people.
Bush honey, wild plum, plenty plum this country.
He been on top, along escarpment there.

Yellow stuff, good one.

. . . . . . . . . . . . . . . . . . . .

People, this one now, what about think about this story?
What about this story, good for you?
Or bad, you don't like him.

He good for you.
Why don't you listen careful.
People like it, white European, tourist.
They want to listen, buy book.
They looking for now.
But what about Aborigine?

You can't forget balanda story.
Balanda story he over us.
Newspaper and telephone and video.
You can look video, picture, TV.
What about Aborigine?
No spear.
No, something more than that.
You make him spear, sell it to white.
'This is my father, grandfather, they used this.'
You can't do it.
You can do it, or no.
Now is no alright.

You got to do something, teach children.
Teach them when they get ten, eleven, might be fifteen.
But I don't know, you don't wake yourself.
They won't get anything.
Anything from your brains, your feeling, yourself.

## OLD MAN'S STORY

Your feeling, you got to go to the feeling of that story.
For story want to turn around, come back to you.
You know that, or no?
You won't see it, but it's there alright.
He go your knowledge, brains, eye.

If you got friend, make him to talk about first.
You two can make it this.
Or get stick and draw something.
Or no, you can't do it, well that mean you can't get anything out of it.
Your kids, they'll be wild.
I know, I see plenty kids.
But I explain this one, explain to you.
Because this story, if you get it, you get it, no-one can stop you.

Painting, you know cave painting, same story.
You go hunting, might be little bit long-necked turtle.
That same story.
You got to eat fish, same story in your feeling.
He come to you.

World, this world, what he give you, give us?
Water; what about feeling?
He come down with rain, or what?
That water, now you got to drink.
He got little medicine for you.
You want water.

Because, other way, if you don't get it, might be mother or father no good.
You miss everything, you don't believe, that's alright, you don't believe.
In you body, that feeling, in your body, string, everything.
You can walk, you can run, what come to you?
He touch you little bit, you feel him, or no?
Oh, my legs, or foot. What's that?

That feeling now, feeling of yourself.
You got to listen all this story.
I suppose, your string, you can walk.
But you might find him something, string on your leg, something sick.
What happens, you'll be crippled, eh?
Walk slow, proper sick.

You won't come back better.
But do it little bit more.
Do little bit more this.
You might keep him, your feeling all clear.
Give you feeling good.
Yourself.

He helping, this water.
Water he come down, give us little bit medicine.

Wind, this wind, he got medicine too.
You might sit down, you won't feel good.
You want this wind, help you.

Me, I feel him meself.
Me inside all the time.
I come out, outside.
I get wind, this one make me good.
Sleep, good sleep.
Big mob sleep, yes.

But what about feeling?
What about story?

This is the one.

OLD MAN'S STORY

## *World like us, we like him*

Old people pointed at plain.
They said, 'Teach people, young.
Young generation, they got to be hunting here.'

'Paintings,' they said, 'leave them for new generation.
Nothing else.
We won't be talking with them, they won't see us.'
This long time, that way they said.

But you look that painting.
He say, 'Ah, he look my painting.'
Well, your feeling, he giving you from that painting.
He give you all that feeling.
If you miss that feeling, something wrong.
Mistake.

But you'll have to get him.
Otherwise too late for you, too late no good.
Sky belong to us, everybody.
World, belong to us.
Much as we want him, they like us.

World like us, we like him.
Don't forget and go something else.
I know, I know this time you forget.
You mob, big mob forget, can't listen.

You got to listen careful, and get feeling of you.
Of that book, or that story.
Get him, and keep him in your feeling.
You can spread out after.
People been start that, old people, old generation.
They said, 'Ah, small painting there for you.'
But he got power; he give you all that.
You got to get him.
But you people, or any people, this time to think about now.
What you want to do?

Because you can't get him anymore.
Something else spoil you.

Well, that's it, he make you think about something else.
You don't think about this one.
What old people, old generation, what they said.
'Keep him all the time, teach children.'

School, they say same way.
But you Aborigine, why you walk away?
No good. You got to do it.

I used to listen careful, now I got him.
For you, might be next day I do little bit more.

I'm trying to put little bit more this one.
For you people.
Because he good for you.
Good for story.
Good for anybody.
Good for you.
Good for me.
Good for somebody.

But if you get him, everybody get him.
And you make him this country normal.
Look better.

. . . . . . . . . . . . . . . . . . . .

Tourists people, they like him, they asking.
But Aborigine, I don't know, I been trying to get couple to make this story.
But nobody.
Why that, because you don't know, or what?
Might be, you don't know your story.

This is my story.
With my father, grandpa, and uncle, everyone.
But your grandpa, your grandad, I'm asking you.
Because your story, I never listen yet.
All my story.

OLD MAN'S STORY

I just fill him in all this, because you don't know.
You people, Aborigine, you never got one story there.
Book, nothing.

You should be make that book.
Get somebody write him out, I tell you mob sixteen year.
But no, something else you think about.
He won't be good, that.
Something else is no good.

He gone now, this one.
You should get him, this story.
Your feeling, your father's feeling, no matter he pass away.
But his skeleton, he's there spirit.
He want to listen to you
Make him better, but no.

My father, he died long time, and mother.
But they can listen to me, what I'm saying.
Uncle, auntie, they listen I'm teaching.
Telling people.
Make them little bit better.
I feel better.

. . . . . . . . . . . . . . . . . . . . .

We took a little pause here while I changed the tape and Old Man took a long swig at the water bottle. Meanwhile, around us on either side of the footy field cars and trucks passed by, and people walked their dogs upon the empty pitch. A police car cruised past, the officers looking suspiciously at our two figures sitting underneath the tree, looking like the drinkers that Old Man referred to so critically.

I felt the poignancy of the situation; Old Man telling his last story upon a footy field in a mining town. He should have been sitting outside the cave at Alamangere where he had told most of his tale, back in his own tribal country, back at Ubirr.

I gave him the signal that I was ready, and then he started the last side.

· · · · · · · · · · · · · · · · · · ·

Way long time ago wasn't any white people here.
Only Aborigine people, like.
What they was doing they was look after country, hunting.
They saved him up, hunting.
They used to mix and save them ground, save him country.
They used to look country same way, helping.

Rock, rock you can't.
They said, 'Ah, that got to be million million year, rock.
So something we can draw.'
Cave.
Well, Ubirr, I was there, and they draw something.

I used to say, 'What's that?'

'Ah, this other people's school, learning, my country look after.'

'But why you mob?
What about you?'

'You won't see us.
Go on, youngfella, go sit down, no more argument.
We're doing this draw.
You learn from us, learning from us.
Just go out, and sit down.
Listen.'

OLD MAN'S STORY

Big mob of them old people.
Spirits.
Old people's spirit, they were there before us.

This is the story.
They never fight their home.
They was save the country.
They used to get him fish.
Enough, they used to eat, no more.
And they save country.

All the time I was there, they teach me.
And I'm teaching you.
Will you do?

If no, you won't get any of this story here.
You'll be nothing left.
You'll have to think about something.
For yourself, or anybody.
This is the one.
Look after country.

## *Alamangere*

You know Alamangere.
I'm talking about Alamangere.
Hill, I'm alongside, sitting down.
There look rock, every morning, afternoon, night.
What that give me?
He give me something, power of that rock.
He don't move, you can't move him.
You can't shift him.
No, that something been leave him there.

That Dalmana.
He been leave him there, rock.
Something got in me, that story, give it to the people.
And people, they got paint there.
What that paint they leave on there?
Rock, you can walk and look rock.
Plenty painting there, you can see something.

Honey, plenty honey there.
Nobody getting it honey.
Something there you drinking, it's not yours.
That silly, make you silly, or you want to fight.

What's the good you want to fight?
Make him bad country.
Your land, you make him bad.
He follow you, him listen to you.

Why don't you settle down.
Talk about something.
Plenty shade.

And somebody coming, like go alonga school.
I said that six year, go longa school for woman.
Talk about and teach him children.
Nobody there.

How do they want to learn?
You tell me, they want to learn by drinking, or what?
Any good, or just fighting?
They listen your fighting.
Kids they know no school.
That not a school, your fighting, killing each other.

You got bandage, hand or finger, that good for you?
Hurt, eh?
Sure.
You go get medicine.

## OLD MAN'S STORY

You ought to leave him medicine.
Because you don't listen.
Why don't you listen?

We explained to you book.
You got to get it.
This book got to be come out later.
I won't be around, you won't be asking me.
Now you can ask me, and I tell you.
Nobody come around, all along a club.

That your story there, club, or fighting?
That your story?
What about old generation to generation?
With this tree, skeleton, what about that story?
What they said uncle, father, mother.
What they was doing, they used to go hunting.
Get yam, honey, porcupine, possum, goanna, all that.

Why don't you do it?

Aborigine, poor thing, all you people, young, they got nothing.
Might be balanda alright, balanda got story.
Balanda making newspaper, everything, any story, TV.
You can't make him TV.
But what about your story?
Just like TV, just like newspaper.

If you do it, you ought to do it, or nothing.
Nothing for kids to learn.
I know already, I can see, you'll be nothing.
Look this country, big country.
Who over there bush, walking around?
Nothing.

They used to walking around before.
Nothing today, all alonga club.
Club is not yours, club for anybody, club for balanda.
Not yours, and make you silly, eh?
You should be think about something else.
Yourself, to teach children.
We sitting on this land, that more important.

Earth important.
He got double double, earth.
He grow you up, earth.
And you got to go back, same place.

The earth should be help you, because country help.
Help country, looking after.
Billabong, plain, plenty fruit, nuts.
You can walk miles and miles and get goanna, long-necked turtle.
Fish, every gully, he got fish.
They just dying, eagle eating it, because you won't go.
Something holding you up.
Silly.

## Go hard way

I used to go cousin.
Talk about skeleton, old people.
They used to take him, make him bunk out there bush.
They used to collect him all that skeleton.
Take him back alonga cave.
What for?
More shade, and dry.

What for a skeleton?
'He'll come back to us.
He'll work with us.
They there.'

## OLD MAN'S STORY

They sit down now, talk about.
And they used to say, 'True alright.'

They been listen, old people.
But we today, you mob, you can't listen.
We explain to you, outside, straight, you can't even listen.
What for?
You ought to listen and think about kids.
What do you want to listen to?
Nothing.

You got no digging stick, nothing.
You got no axe.
Better axe this time, white man, good axe.
You can chop him honey more quick.
That old people they had stone axe.
They used to climb, and make a hollow there, and get him out honey.
That hard work, eh?
You can't climb top, but old people, they used to climb.
You mob, nothing.

No matter you go shop, that balanda, that one, easy one.
Go hard way, hunting, bush, get honey.

You can walk.
But you won't go, I never seen one go.
We getting honey from balanda.
Why don't you get him bush honey?
Belong to us, you can eat, and teach.

Cut him honey, cut him down, that's the one.
And country, look after.
You not looking for honey.
Honey might be waiting there, but you can't.

Bush fruit.
If you need bush fruit, will you get him?
And look, what you want to do?
He won't kill you, fruit.
But you, you don't like.
But that fruit he got flavour.

I know everyone bread and butter.
I know that.
But try bush, he make you more lively.
In our feeling, he got stuff.

They told me, my people, old people.
They told me everything.

## *Dream*

You dream something.
He come to you.

We too, come to you, and tell you, 'Hey, you got to dream.'
He's there. You got to dream something.
You got to dream might be bad dream.

If good one, all the dream good one, you like it that dream.
You don't have to tell us, or tell somebody.
Because that dream he run away from you.

More better, you keep him, so he can dream again.
Because he'll belong your feeling, body.
No matter how much you can say.
But he's true, you can dream again.

That dream might like you.
But if you tell other man, or other woman, he run away.

He go other man or woman.

OLD MAN'S STORY

## *Pick him up story*

Country.
Big country this one Kakadu, big one.
That rock, all the rock there, he go right along.
All the story up there, skeleton.

But why don't you go there, look, and pick him up story.
No, you don't leave, you can't go, you stay one place.
Well, kids can't learn anything.

Skeleton.
You can't talk about skeleton, but they there.
Tree, you say tree dead.
Tree, he working for you, help you.

Young tree, old tree.
That old one over there, dry, that's just about like me.
Might be next year he'll fall down, strong wind.
All same.
Because tree, close up like man.

Animal, no animals, eh?
Because you're too slack, if you tell plenty story, animals they come back.
They listening, any animal, no matter who animal.

Fish, you think about fish.
Why don't you talk about more, or you leave it.
When you leave it, the fish he go back weak, like yourself.

If you happy, talk about river, creek, billabong.
I tell you all day, two or three day.
When you go down billabong, ah! fish everywhere!
That story help.

Crow, that skeleton people, all been dead.
Crow, that the one, old people.
That one crow, he come talk to us.

And now what, Marrawaddi, eagle.
That our father, if you get story.
You say bird, 'Ah, go away.'
You silly, that our father.

Jabiru, he tell you where that fish.
He looking for fish.
You go look jabiru, 'Ah, fish there, I'll go.'
He man.
This jabiru now, he fly from that way.
Jabiru him here.

You people, you not learning that.
Another way around you want to learn.
Time for you, I think look like late now.
Too late, I suppose.
Getting late.

You might look this book, and listen something.
Read it, because you nothing left.
Nothing, you can't do anything.
You might listen.
You might read it.
Somebody will.

What this story?
Story should be for you, teaching other people.
Old people, they listen to you.
You got to ask old people, 'I want to do this one.'
'Ma, you try.'
But you don't do one bit.

But more better, I see you.
I say, 'Book, might be, you might look.'
But you, nothing.

OLD MAN'S STORY

I see plenty people, woman, man, young.
Nothing, no story.
What for?
What learn?
You got to help learn, look after.

Skeleton, he follow you people.
But the skeleton, what they said, 'We got to go, finish.
But we can't see our people, we blocked.
We can't come back, learn and look them.
We should be do that, but we blocked.'

They in the bush, they watching us.
Good man, they used to come and talk to him.
Or clap him stick.
Signal, clapstick, or bamboo, you can listen.
He giving you more power.
But you don't do anything.
You don't do any good.
If you do any good, he help you.

Land help you, too.

## Make a story

This earth, big country, Karraba, yeah.
I call him Karraba, land we sitting on.
You want to look after; you got to look after your country.
Other people they got to do same way, might be.
Twenty years time, you come together, big ceremony, good one.
I been waiting for you mob.
But no, I'm doing meself, little bit.
Better.

White people, they like him, but you mob, you forget.
You forget your culture, all that, is it that true?
I got him, mine, culture, and I can tell you.
I know already, I can see you, I can see you empty.
Your brains, nothing, knowledge nothing.
What you want to do?
Just gooooo, finish.

I just want to say the end of it.
Your country, I'm talking about your country, my country.
I'm looking after there, but you people, you can do that, or no.
I see already, Jabiru, they miss.

But you got to help little bit your country, and make a story.
But no, you don't like, or you don't like talk.
Because, end of it, this one I'm just saying, might be end.
Might be it'll be finish, my story, and end of it is nothing.
Nothing for you.
You should be carrying on something, your story.
Another twenty year, you can make him.
Me, too late.
Country important, your father story, auntie story, mother, uncle.
And country.

## *Look after country, like I been done*

Look after country, like I been done.
I used to look after country.
He's alright, but you, plenty people you, you should help.
You should help.

Biggest country, this.
Earth, same way earth.
But we can't get there too far earth, because long way to jump.

## OLD MAN'S STORY

That story nearly finish, end of it.
Might be not you mob.
But might be people, balanda, they might read it.

Look grass there.
Nobody on that side, good side there.
Nobody sit down there, talking something.
Should be sit down there.
Talk, and making basket, something.
That your partner, making something, help you out.
And he help you, sky, and earth.
World, I mean.
But you can't do.
You don't do anything.

So I'm going, end of it, nearly finished, but warning you.
What about that you forget?
Forget your culture, what you want to do?

Your father, auntie, they heard that story, every one of them.
And you young, and kids, you got nothing.
That funny, no good.
Very bad for you.

You should be look after country.
Land, trees, save him country, save him tree.
Grow more trees might be, shade, you should be.
Look after grass, look grass green, soon it'll be dry.
Who got to be look after?
Balanda.
You, nothing.
What for?
What that?
Why you don't look after?

You're killing your land.
Land, this country, big country.
But you killing by your feeling.
If you wake, he'll wake.
Making him happy.
And you'll be happy yourself.

You don't know that one, eh?
You might say, 'That I can't do.'
That mean you don't know nothing.

If you help your country, he help you.
Tree, grass, you don't believe that, but he will, he will help you.

But you, I don't know you kids, what got to be happen?
Something got to be happen this country.
But little bit balanda they look after, help you, run around.

If this Jabiru finish, what you want to do?
Nothing, you'll be dead, eh? Or what?
Children get weak and weak, that's it, or no.
You will.
Too hard, the feeling, or knowledge, too hard for you.
If you don't understand, very bad.
You should understand.

## *World work with us*

World.
World working with us, work with you.
You don't think about that, you don't know, so you killing land.

What you want to do?
You want to think about something, or leave it?
Bad, very bad, no good, I'm telling you, I can see already.
I'm in Jabiru, I can see already.

## OLD MAN'S STORY

You think I'm sitting down, sleep.
What I doing?
I think about you.

I think about what you want to do.
I see plenty youngfellas, they don't teach, explain, nothing.
Youngfellas, walking around.
Well, you start killing now.

What you want to do?
What you want to eat?
What the old way?
All the old time?
Hunting.
You left that, you don't know.

I used to go hunting, teaching children.
And all the children they know.
When I bring them in here, Jabiru, they go little bit drink.
They go mad.

I said, 'Alright, bad place.
Take away to Cannon Hill.
They won't think about drink.
They go hunting.'

Your uncle and auntie, what they was doing here?
They was go hunting, way over there, rock, get wallaby.
They used to come back with wallaby, bush honey.
And what about this time?
Nothing.

You go easy way, hard way, you left it.
Why don't you go hard way?
Exercise, get your knowledge back.
Nothing, what for?

Who's stopping you?
Yourself.

The story, he good for you, yourself and kids.
Somebody can listen to you.
Somebody can explain to you, talk over.
Or no, you don't like.
What you want to do?

He's waiting, waiting for you, waiting for us.
I only one man, I got little bit name there, making story.
And they like him, should be more.
You mob, your language, your country, your painting.
Might be painting there, river. You don't do that, what for?
You ought to do it, he good for you.
River, he help you too.

Why the wind blowing?
What he do to you?
Wind got little bit medicine there, people like it, I like him.
But what about you?
You don't know wind.
What for? People like it, wind.
Good for them, and good for me.

And you other, you don't like him.
What for?
You ought to shame yourself.
Hot, got to be hot, because you no good half, he follow you.
But you got to listen.
Listen; think about something hard, what you want to do?

That why I'm telling you.
What you want to do with kids, your children, what you want to see?
You might kill this land, you will see nothing.

If you wake up, see.
Better for you.

That way they done, old people.
Old generation, they said, well look after.
No matter, we'll be dead, skeleton, we'll come back.
Because they need this country, they was telling me big story.
I was laying down.
Star, they told me everything.

I don't see you, you don't like world, you don't like water.
Well, you no good, no good for you.
You can't do it.

That way I said, you got lot of family, sisters, brother, cousin, daughter, son.
What got to be that mob?
You got plenty, well good for you.
You can tell him, you got chance.
Chance for you, your time.

Might be you go ahead, you get better than me.

Story, I still winning, I got everything.
My story I putting in this little tape, he won't hurt you.
And people can write it down after.
You speak English, why don't you do it?

## *Mother and father*

You people like, you don't think about what's going on.
Old people and country, well look after.
Well look after your father.
You think about your father, what he done.
He dead.

Few, few people, I seen it already, daughter, son.
You never help.
You never help your mother, you never help your father.

Daughter, son, must look after.
Look after your mother, where you grow up?
You grow from belly, you outside now, laying down.
You should help your mother, no matter how much.
You can do it, but you don't do it.
Funny.
Funny people.

You want to do what she been do, help you to grow up.
She never leave you on the ground, she save your life.
Mother is mother.
Father, that's the one important that, he grow you up.

Mother and father, when they gone away, auntie, same way, she look after you.
Give you little bit knowledge.
They teach me, I try teach you.

But I don't know, wind blowing, him strong.
Because they listen my story, eh?
And blowing more hard, when I'm gone.

## *Wake yourself*

This is the story, nearly end of it.
But I explained to you, will you wake yourself?
Do something, or no?
If doesn't matter now, that's alright with you, you killing country.
Your country you killing, you kill your country, that true.

Nearly end of it.
Yes, well look after your father and mother, how you grow.
I know, old man, he was feeding you.
Put you name, telling you story.
And you never say, 'Ah, my father country, little bit help.
Help this country, what my father been here.'

## OLD MAN'S STORY

You can't do it?
What for?
You should be help.
It's your country, every land each.
Land claim, all that, you got him.
You just leave him.
What for?
No matter he buried.
You can tell him story, him listen to you.

Even your mother, she dead alright, skeleton.
But there, watching you, but you no good.
Well, she walk away, she listening.
No matter how, or where you go.
You can't tell me that nobody around.
Hah! they there, you don't know.

What happen me, they told me same thing.
I listen, alright.

You don't listen.

I been run away.
And I believe.
Next day a dream, no I been dream.
And he's true.
I said true alright.
You mob, you can do that?
I know you don't believe me.
Balanda they listen.
They believe me.

Country.
The earth, big place this one.
And world, big one.
Who that for?
Not ourself.
Everyone.
No matter what colour.
Everybody.
No matter where from.

You got to do it.
If nothing, you can't do it anything, bad luck for you.
It'll be bad luck, I say.

Plenty already, now I been look.
You'll be bad luck.
You don't know this story what I'm saying.
You don't like it, yeah, you don't like.
Well yourself, you'll be weared out yourself.
You'll be finish.
Finish.

*At this point I signalled Old Man that the tape was coming to the end, and that he should finish soon.*

## OLD MAN'S STORY

Well, end of it now.
You know what I said, youngfellas.
Might be you mob got to be happen like that.
Because you haven't got story on you.
So, might be something happen.

End of it, this one.
Because you won't see me.
But you can look book.
This is the end of it, I say.

Good job I had good friend.
And we, I just been filling in this story.
All the rest, he'll work it out himself.

But, I'm saying is, end of it now.
I finish all my story.
But, that why I said, hard, will you think about?
Do something for your children, and young.
And youngfellas, they should get him.
This story important for you.
For anybody.

So, I'm just about finish now, no more.
That's all.

No more.

# BACK TO THE DRY

## OLD MAN'S STORY

Knock 'em down storm crossing floodplain.

It was April, the Wet Season was coming to an end, and the rain fell less frequently. The speargrass, which had covered the ground with a green velvety fuzz at the start of the Wet, now grew taller than a man.

This was the season of the 'knock 'em downs' — sudden storms where the skies would darken and swirling towers of cloud swept across the country carried on roaring winds which whipped through the bush, breaking the slender stems of the speargrass, literally knocking them down into a jumbled thicket.

These storms, and the thousands of tiny dragonflies that had hatched and now filled the air with their frantic buzzing, heralded the end of the Wet.

Old Man viewed the storms with relief, for they also signalled the end of his time in Jabiru. Soon he would be free to return to his country. I would be gone from here too. My sister in England was getting married and I should fly back there for the wedding.

I spent my last days in Jabiru writing up the text from Old Man's tapes, and this I took around to show him before I said goodbye. He was concerned that

I might be gone for good, but I told him that I would return before too long because there was more work for me to do here. I had many more pictures of his country to take, for any book with the story that he had told me would have to be illustrated, and the time that I had spent here already had shown me how many more moods the country had.

So I would be back.

'You just make sure you're still here when I return, Old Man,' I said.

'Yer, right, might be,' he said, lip stuck out, tilting a hand from side to side.

He extended a skinny hand and said softly, 'Goodbye, friend.'

'Goodbye, Old Man. Now, do you want me to bring you anything back from England?'

'Yer, pipe, might be, please.'

'But I bought you a pipe already when I was in Melbourne! What happen to that one?'

'I had good friend come say hello last weekend. He like that pipe, so…'

OLD MAN'S STORY

I chided him, 'You're bloody hopeless, Old Man. That was a good pipe that one. Alright, I bring you another one, and write your name on it, so no bugger can humbug you again.'

'Right, ma, thank you.'

'And I'll bring a tin of Irish tobacco. Them Irish, they're storytellers too, you know.'

'Right, good one, I better still be here,' he smirked.

\*\*\*

Two months later, I flew back to Darwin and drove into Kakadu and made for East Alligator immediately, back to his old house.

He was sitting cross-legged upon his bed, a cheeky welcome upon his face.

'How you, Old Man?'

'Gooooood,' he rumbled, 'how you?'

'All the better for seeing you. Here, I bought you this.'

I handed him a new Peterson pipe with a silver cap upon its stem on which were deeply engraved in large capital letters: 'BILL NEIDJIE', and a tin of dark Irish tobacco which he asked me to crumble up and put into the pipe.

'This is storytellers tobacco, Old Man. Only storytellers can smoke him.'

He lit up the pipe and disappeared into a cloud of blue smoke, emerging like a genie.

'Mmmm, goooood! Anyone take this pipe, I kill him,' he growled, flexing his long arms.

Later I went around to the cave where the old spirits lived, to say hello again. I sat on the ground and leaned my back against the wall under the painting of the Rainbow Serpent, the creative spirit, and asked for some help in the times ahead. The birds called through the trees. It was good to be back.

I spent that night at the nearby campground and made a quiet fire beside which I lay my swag, and slept under the clear stars, the moon shining through the woollybutt trees silhouetted against the sky. As the 'buk buk' owls called softly in the darkness I thought of how Old Man must be so relieved to be back in his country.

This would be my spot, too. Here I would camp for the next few months.

There were a few new faces besides the old crew up at the Ranger Station. Trevor was back from London to work another season as a Ranger, but the contract for art site surveillance was now in the hands of Lisa at the Border Store, the little shop near the entrance gate to Ubirr. Darrin was installed in a house with Casey, an Aboriginal Ranger. Their freezer was a lot like Old Man's fridge; a dead animal was likely to be staring out at you from the icy interior as you opened the door looking for the milk. Casey was a cheerful, shy and quietly-spoken man, and he loved Old Man dearly.

'He like a father to me,' he explained, softly.

And there was Jo. Old Man had mentioned Jo.

'Good woman, that one,' he had boomed.

Jo was an ex-nurse who was now working as a Seasonal Ranger, and she and Old Man had taken a great liking to each other. She was a straight-shooter like most nurses are, with a silly sense of humour and a big heart, and I liked her right away.

Trevor was ferreting around in his caravan making the place nice and tidy, ready for the impending arrival of his girlfriend Angela, who was due to fly in from London in the next couple of days. She had a job arranged already; for Lisa was looking for someone to look after surveillance at Ubirr.

I was tempted to apply for my old job, but no, I had other work to do, so I made a home in the local campground. By hanging a truck tarpaulin from some of the trees and setting a large mozzie dome underneath in the shade, I made ready for a long stay.

Old Man had mentioned that he would like to camp out with us, one night soon. There was a full moon due the next week, and, as it was the Dry Season there would be no risk of rain, so as long as Old Man was feeling good, we could go.

When the day came he was raring to go, waiting in his wheelchair out on the verandah. I sat him in the truck and we drove through the bush following a vague track to a clearing among some outliers. There were even more paintings here, and a campsite with a beautiful spreading tree with soft sand underneath, a perfect spot. We sat him down on a blanket upon the sand, I got a fire going and stirred a stew that I had made earlier; Old Man's nostrils flaring in anticipation. As the flames crackled the full moon rose through the trees, the stars glittering above us.

Old Man pointed to Mars.

'That red one, he that eye, King Brown Snake,' he said, and moving his hand towards the Pleiades, 'Seven Sister, they over there.'

'What you call the Southern Cross, Old Man?' someone asked.

'Crocodile and spear,' he said, his eyes glinting in the firelight.

Here he was, the storyteller, surrounded by his eager listeners.

He had a story of travelling with a missionary through this country in the early days. They had come to a creek, and the missionary said that he would camp close to the water. Old Man had said that was not a good idea and that he should come and camp with him beside the fire, away from the creek and the crocodiles.

'No, my Jesus look after me. I'll camp here by the water,' the missionary insisted.

'Hmm, please yourself, but I camp over there. You should camp there too.'

The missionary remained where he was.

In the middle of the night a shrill scream woke Bill from his slumber and he rushed to the waterside to wrench the missionary's leg from out the jaws of a large crocodile. However, being the strong man that he was, he managed to throw the missionary some distance, so that the man fell badly, breaking his arm. He was incensed and not at all grateful that Bill had saved his life.

'I reckon his Jesus not much chop,' said Bill with a frown, 'all this business,' he grunted, crossing himself approximately. But worst of all, when they reached civilisation, the missionary had not mentioned a word of what had occurred; concerned that he might have appeared foolish.

'Rubbish man, that one,' said Old Man with a spit in the dark.

Old Man yawned into the fire. We laid out a swag and hung a mosquito net from the branches of the tree and made him comfortable for the night.

Jo slept nearby.

I crept into the truck and slipped into sleep.

In the wee small hours there was a call from Old Man.

'Jo, hey Jo!'

He was cold, freezing cold. We were all out of our swags, and gathered as much firewood as we could find. These days he had so little flesh on him that he really felt the cold. We built up the cooking fire, then started a fire on the other side of him, but he was still shivering, and by the time we were finished, he had four fires burning around him.

Then the moon set, the eastern sky blushed pink, and the day dawned, so we moved Old Man into the shade of the tree, out of the heat of the sun. We were tired, we'd had very little sleep, so we moved around camp like zombies, packing the gear up ready to go back to work, gently rousing Old Man from his sleep to take him back to his house and put him to bed, wrapped up warm.

We were a quiet little mob, but we were happy, for we'd camped the night out together under the stars, beside the fire with Old Man.

\*\*\*

The Dry Season mornings could be chilly, and foggy too. A cold snap three weeks later hit Old Man hard and he went down badly with the flu. I called in to the house to see if there was anything I could do. He was sitting bent in his wheelchair, moaning softly.

'I'm no good,' he groaned.

'Has Doctor seen you, Old Man?' I asked.

'Yer, but tablets they no good, ring Doctor, tell him please,' he whispered.

I scurried round to the Ranger Station and rang the clinic in Jabiru.

Doctor Klaas said that there was nothing more they could do; he'd given Old Man injections and a full complement of tablets already. All he could recommend was that he keep taking the pills that he had prescribed until they were finished. I reported back to Old Man, who just nodded, resigned to his fate.

'They do me no good. Nothing, no good.'

His eyes were back in his head like he was punch-drunk. I was worried for him.

'What happen old people's time? What would they give you?' I asked.

'Too hard,' he mumbled, but I could see he was thinking about my question.

He raised his head and said, 'Turtle egg and sugarbag might be good.'

I waited in silence for some more information as he gathered his breath.

'If I could get that sugarbag, I'd be better tomorrow.'

'Right, Old Man, we find you that sugarbag.'

Sugarbag is honey from the local bees who make their hives in the hollows of the woollybutt trees, all of which were now in blossom. I thought that the one person I could rely upon to find some sugarbag for Old Man would be Casey, so I made my way round to his house that evening. Casey was cooking some fish when I knocked on his door. He asked me to join him for a feed and to sit around his fire, which he started with four matches, struck, and then thrown like darts on all four sides.

'I like an even-burning fire,' he grinned.

## OLD MAN'S STORY

I sat beside him and explained that Old Man was crook and was asking for sugarbag. Casey's face grew more and more serious. He picked up the phone and rang the boss to tell him he would be out looking for sugarbag first thing tomorrow. Old Man was seriously ill and was asking for it, and so he'd be in to work a little late.

Then he rubbed his hands with glee.

Any excuse to go and spend some time in the bush!

At first light we loaded my truck with a couple of axes and a plastic bag to carry the honeycomb, and took the track out to the forest near Cannon Hill, looking for a trail of bees heading for a tree hollow. We looked here, we looked there, we looked everywhere; not a sign did we see.

We drove round to the small community of Cannon Hill and asked some of Old Man's family to come with us, and even with their help we had no joy.

Casey's boss came on the radio to tell him was needed back at the workshop, so we had to call off the search and return back to base.

We'd left that morning without any breakfast, so I drove up to the Border Store for a pie and a milkshake as my guts were rumbling with hunger. Lisa was her normal cheerful self, and asked me why I looked so glum. I told her of our fruitless morning.

'Couldn't find any sugarbag!' she chortled. 'I've got some in the bloody front yard!'

'Naah, I don't believe you,' I protested.

'No mate, come and have a look,' she said, pulling me by the sleeve to a small garden that bordered the outside tables. There on the ground was a big black honeycomb with tiny bees buzzing all around it. Maybe it fell from out of one of the trees.

Old Man's youngest daughter Elizabeth came sauntering into the shop.

'Hey, Elizabeth, is this sugarbag?' I asked.

'Yer, that sugarbag,' she grinned her enormous smile.

'Right you are then,' said Lisa, 'I'll get you a bucket.'

I shovelled the honeycomb into the bucket and the bees swarmed around me angrily, but they were a stingless variety so they were just like a cloud of tiny flies.

I lashed the bucket to the roof-rack, and with Elizabeth on board we drove back to the house with a trail of bees following behind us like an angry wind.

Old Man was slumped in his wheelchair. I gently shook him from his sleep.

'We found you that sugarbag, Old Man, you want to try him?'

'Yer,' he stirred, 'give me here.'

I broke up the honeycomb on a dustbin lid and squeezed the honey out of the comb and into a cup. He drank that, and then took the comb and slurped away at the earthy wax where the yellow blobs of pollen hung loose, honey dripping down his chin.

'Gooood,' he said, as he licked his chops.

'Right, Old Man, we try and find you some more.'

After that, the family went searching for sugarbag in the trees.

I went round to the house the next day to see if Old Man was feeling any better, and Simon, one of his grandsons, came running up to me.

'Hey, Mark, you got axe?'

'Yeah, in the back of the truck!'

'Quick, give me, I found sugarbag! Big one!'

I handed him the axe and he bounded away over the rocks and returned proudly carrying a buzzing trophy, licking his fingers. He handed it over to Old Man who took it gratefully. Simon beamed, and handed me back the axe, grinning his thanks.

I could see that Old Man was pleased that his young people had gone into the bush to look for the sugarbag, and found it too, lots of it. There were echoes of the story that he had told me of looking for sugarbag himself when he was a youngfella, and how pleased he had been when he finally found it.

Needless to say, a few days later, the old fella was as right as rain.

*** 

However, Old Man's bout of the flu got me thinking. What would happen to all of this story when he passed away?

In some Aboriginal cultures when somebody dies you cannot mention that person's name, or show a picture of them. In the short time that I had been in Kakadu one notable person had died already, and the locals would refer to him as 'that young fella who lived down Jim Jim way', rather than by his name.

What would happen to Old Man's spirit when I produced a book of his words with pictures of him within its pages? What would happen to the portraits of Old Man that I had shot? Would they all have to be destroyed or hidden away?

There was only one person I should ask. I felt that was a very delicate matter however, and I was frankly nervous about discussing it with him.

I walked round to the house in the mid-afternoon, and Old Man was sitting in front of the television, his nose inches away from the screen. Gene Kelly was dancing among a throng of leggy blondes, their petticoats flashing, and Old Man was enthralled, so I had to wait until the commercial break before we could talk.

'I'm sorry to disturb you Old Man, but I got difficult question.'

'Right, take me round other side, nice and quiet there.'

I wheeled him to the other side of the house, out on the verandah.

'Old Man, I been thinking, what happen to all this story, all them pictures what we done, when, you, you know… er…'

'When I been pass away?'

'Well, yes.'

'Hmm, no matter,' he calmly announced.

'But what happen that old Law, Aborigine Law, you can't talk about someone when they been pass away. You can't say his name. You got to hide that picture. What going to be happen to your story?'

'No matter, he alright. That not Law business, that culture one, that one.'

'Right,' I sighed with relief, 'so this story what we done, he's safe alright.'

'Yer, sure,' he nodded.

'Them pictures, I can show them. That book, I can make him. No bugger can say I done wrong thing.'

'Yeah, no matter, he alright.'

'Ah good, I was worried, might be we done all this work for nothing.'

He had a little think.

'Well, best job, you make piece of paper to say that thing, and I sign him.'

'Right, Old Man, I do that one.'

'Ma, good one, thank you, I see you.'

'Boh boh, Old Man, thank you.'

And he wheeled himself back to the whirling girlies.

***

It was early September, and another of Old Man's friends had passed away, a man with whom he shared the responsibility of looking after one of the most sacred places to be found in his country: Injuwanydjuwa, a vast rock shaped like a man that stood alone in the midst of a billabong covered with red waterlilies, hidden away behind the massif of Cannon Hill. It was a very sacred place and no-one was allowed there on their own.

Old Man had wanted to take me there, had wanted to see that place again himself, but we had got severely bogged on our way there, and then had to be towed out by the Rangers who had followed us in case we ran into trouble.

He went to the funeral of his old friend, and I left him in peace for a few days so that he could mourn, for they had been very close. However, I saw two of his grandsons, Simon and James, after the funeral. They were really excited for they had both been ceremonially painted-up with ochre for the first time in their lives so that they could dance for that old man at his funeral, and the experience had affected them greatly.

I asked them if they could take me out to Injuwanydjuwa, and camp out there overnight during the next full moon; something I knew I could not ask Old Man to do for he was far too fragile. They both agreed but said they would have to talk to Old Man first, just to make sure.

Within a few days, all was arranged.

I had to hire a helicopter to fly us in, for there was a tributary of the river to cross, and the Rangers had warned me that there was a monster crocodile that inhabited that waterway, so I was not disposed to be crossing it in a small boat. I asked Old Man about that crocodile, and he said, 'Well, respect that old fella. But don't think about him too much, or you call him up and bring him to you.'

So I trusted in the old spirits to look after us.

As the full moon approached James had to go to Oenpelli to spend time with his family, but Simon was keen to go.

The chopper picked us up from the Cannon Hill airstrip on a clear evening, and it was only a short hop across the country, but my heart was beating fast. I was entering a special sacred place where many people were buried. As soon as we had landed, unloaded our gear and carried it up onto the safety of a large sandstone ledge, Simon sang out in language to the old spirits that lived there to say hello, and to ask them for their protection while we were in their country.

Above our campsite, painted in yellow ochre upon the smooth rock face was the figure of Injuwanydjuwa himself, the creative being who, in the local

OLD MAN'S STORY

Injuwanydjuwa by moonlight.

Aboriginal belief, formed this landscape. When he had completed all of his tasks he had turned himself into the vast rock which stood there below us among the waterlilies in the gathering gloom.

Simon made camp while I climbed down and set up the camera behind the tall palms that grew there, well way from the water's edge, for I felt that I was being watched by eyes unseen. The evening sky darkened into the deepest blue, and then the bright yellow disc of the full moon rose over the Arnhem Land escarpment. The light breeze fell to a whisper and the moonlight shone upon the ripples of the billabong, the leaves of the waterlilies rattling softly.

In the darkness the silhouette of the rock became even more like that of a motionless giant asleep in an endless dream, tiny wavelets lapping at his flanks. I took my pictures quietly and joined Simon beside a small fire back up on the rock ledge; both of us spoke in whispers.

Somewhere in the distance, dingoes howled. This was no place to be, out here on your own.

The moon was higher now and shone down upon the mirrored surface of the water surrounding the figure of Injuwanydjuwa with a rim of shimmering silver, and in the midst of this spectre of light there appeared a huge crocodile's head. Just the eyes, ears and the tip of his snout broke the water as he slowly cruised past us, a pinprick of light reflected in his eye from the flames of our fire. He was watching us. We had felt his eyes upon us as soon as we arrived.

Simon said that he only had one arm and had lived there forever; a guardian to that sacred rock. As we stared down at him, a low rumble, a growl as deep as thunder, rose from the water. Then another head appeared, and this cruised past us too, but it was smaller than the huge head that we had first seen. This would be the monster crocodile's female. There was a swirl of water and a blowing of bubbles, and the low, growling bellow again. The female floated past us, going the other way, out into the open water of the billabong, and shortly after the huge male's head followed.

OLD MAN'S STORY

We saw no more of them that night, only sensed their presence. Now and then there would be that ominous rumble out there in the night, against the shrilling of crickets and the lowing of the cattle across the river.

We ate our dinner by the light of the fire, and turned in early as the mosquitos fell upon us.

I was up at the first sign of dawn, and returned to where I was the previous evening to shoot the scene by the early light as egrets and flocks of magpie geese flew across the scarlet sky. Two cormorants alighted upon the head of that old rock, white with droppings, and watched the water for any sign of fish. Simon crept down to the water's edge and tossed in a handline, but I was very relieved when he called it a day, for I could still feel that old crocodile around us out there in the water.

Later in the day when we had explored the cliffs behind us, Simon said, 'Now I'm going to take you to a special place where we put Old Man, one day.'

With my heart in my mouth I followed him through the bush until we came to a small cave. Simon indicated with a silent gesture for me to look within.

There, placed back in the gloom, were the bones and skulls of the old people; their final resting place. One day soon, Old Man would rest here, too.

Above us a hawk circled, around and around, like a sentinel.

Later in the day Simon returned to the billabong to try for an evening fish while I sat on the rocks nearby and absorbed the immensity of what I had just seen. I walked a little way beside the shallow water to where a rock provided a seat from which to keep an eye on Simon as he cast his line beside the water's edge. Beyond him, the hunched figure of Injuwanydjuwa stood in the water among the waterlilies. From where I sat, he looked even more like an old man, standing there in the billabong.

But more than that. With his head white from the bird droppings, his profile looked just like Old Man himself, with his white hair, his lower lip pushed out, like when he was pointing. And so it suddenly occurred to me that Old Man's spirit and Injuwanydjuwa would one day be together, right here. How appropriate that this sacred place was where he would finally rest; a spirit come home to the heart of his country.

My reverie was broken by a cry from Simon as he hauled in a big fish from the billabong. It lay flapping upon the rocks, the light in its green eye reflecting the sinking sun. I made a fire, and the moon rose into the dark sky of night as we sat on the warm rocks and cooked our fish, and felt the presence of the old people sitting there with us. Long ago they had sat here too.

It seemed that out here beside the billabong, in the shade of Injuwanydjuwa, time had slipped away. The rock stood in the water, impassive as a statue, the waves quietly lapping. In this special place, past, present and future were all one. An endless dream. I thanked Simon for such a special day, and slipped into a moonlit sleep.

The chopper landed after first light, and dropped us back into the other world.

\*\*\*

Days later the Olympics opened in Sydney, and that evening Trevor and Angela invited several of us around to watch the Opening Ceremony. It was a heartening experience to sit with them and our Aboriginal mates to watch as a tribal elder led a young girl by the hand through a Dreamtime world, revealing to her a spectre of bushfire and rejuvenation as a new world emerged from the ashes.

It seemed to champion the hope that a young spirit, young as the nation of Australia, might learn from the wisdom of the elders and our past.

It was a rousing moment to see Cathy Freeman, an Aboriginal athlete, hold the flame aloft. By evening's end the whole of humankind seemed represented by the nations gathered in the arena, and you could only hope and pray that one day we could dwell in harmony and peace with each other, in peace upon this planet.

Watching those dancing figures, you might almost feel this could be so.

\*\*\*

Old Man's health was faring well until he took a chill and was confined to his bed. The Rangers were worried that they might have to fly him out to Darwin. I crept round to see him. Casey and Darrin were sitting beside him, and their faces were creased with concern. There was an oxygen mask upon his face and the Doctor from Jabiru was taking his pulse. His breathing was laboured and faint. The house was quiet and the family stood in the shadows, watching. We all held a vigil in our hearts for him, hoping that he would rally, yet again.

That afternoon I walked up to Ubirr and photographed the dark wings of cloud as they flew over the floodplain. As I waited for another storm to approach I saw a solitary jabiru, a black and white heron, standing alone upon a distant rock looking back towards where Old Man lay. I trained my binoculars upon him, and it almost seemed as if he stood there like a spirit bird, waiting. As I watched him in that tight circle of view, another jabiru flew into the frame alighting upon

## OLD MAN'S STORY

the same rock, and they both opened their wings in greeting to each other. My heart was beating, there were tears in my eyes. Was this Old Man's father come to take his spirit back home? Had he passed away?

The two birds flew off together, and I watched them without blinking as they wheeled through the stormy sky and swooped down to the rainforest, down to the gleaming water, until they disappeared from view. I left soon after, and with a sense of foreboding called round to the house.

The family must have read my face.

'He alright, he's a little better,' they told me.

I left him alone for a few days until I got word that he was feeling a lot stronger. I told him that I had been worried when I saw the jabirus up at Ubirr that he might have passed away, but he smiled, shook his head, and said, 'No, me still here, eh.'

'So what totem you got Old Man? What animal is your animal?'

'Crow, might be,' he said, 'crow is old people's spirit, and I'm old people.'

'Right, I remember that one, Old Man.'

I was due to go to Darwin for a last visit to the dentist, so after we had chatted for a while I asked him if he needed anything in Darwin.

'Yes, mosquito net please, this one, he's all buggered up,' he said.

'No worries, Old Man, I find you proper good one.'

I left the chore until the last moment, and it was upon a Darwin Sunday that I ventured out. I had to return on the Greyhound bus to Jabiru at dawn the next morning and all the shops were closed, save the supermarkets and the chain stores.

I looked high and low, but the only mosquito net that I could find would have suited a Virgin Princess; with its bamboo hoop at the top hanging from the delicate peak it looked almost medieval. I bought it anyway; I couldn't return empty-handed.

I hung it above Old Man's bed and his family cracked up laughing.

Old Man looked like Othello in the bed of the Fairie Queen.

\*\*\*

Late one golden afternoon, I found Old Man sitting alone in his wheelchair at the Border Store, and so I sat down with him. I told him that I didn't know where I would go next. After I had finished here, where would my home be? He told me that my country would call me, for that was what had happened to him.

'I didn't believe it when old people told me that, but he's true alright,' he said, nodding wisely. 'Your country, he call you. That tree, he'll call you in the night.'

His eyes were glistening, and I knew I need not worry.

I remembered an occasion when I had sat with him looking through a book that depicted the work of Donald Thomson, a man who had spent a lot of time in Arnhem Land in the earlier part of the century. One particular picture had affected Old Man greatly. He had stared at it for a long time. It showed a young tribesman lying prone upon the ground and the man was crying, for he had only just returned to his tribal country after being away from it for a very long while.

'I know how that fella was feeling,' Old Man said, patting the page gently. 'When I was away from here, my country was singing out for me, and when I come back here, this was how I was feeling too.'

His words stayed with me as I walked back to the campground through the forest of woollybutts and stringybark trees that bordered the path, and I felt like I walked through a throng of friends, each a silent, watching spirit.

It seemed appropriate that I should try and capture this feeling in a picture.

One of these friends might call me home, one day.

OLD MAN'S STORY

Spirit Tree in the morning light.

The dawn was cold, and the sky clear. A few clouds passed lazily across the morning sun, and the light was beautiful as it sparkled through the dew.

As the kookaburras called I was out of my swag and onto the pushbike, looking for a tree somewhere in the forest that might resemble a human form, personifying the idea of a spirit.

It was there down by the creek: a beautiful smooth white gumtree, standing with pale, slender arms outstretched, as if in greeting, the early sun shining through the grass behind it in a blaze of golden light.

As I photographed it, I thought of Old Man's words:

'Your country, he call you.

That tree, he'll call you in the night.'

Old Man had a visitor come and stay, one of his oldest friends from early days, Tiger. He had often talked of the journeys that they had made together, just the two of them, journeys of several hundred kilometres; walking down to Katherine, up to Cobourg.

I went to the house to say hello, anticipating a man of some stature. Instead Tiger was stocky with a tubby little body, a small beard and wispy hair, but he was animated and chatty. He had brought his wife Dolly with him too. They also had their five dogs with them; they and the three dogs that currently lived at Old Man's place circled each other warily as the evening meal cooked upon the fire.

Dolly was tired from the journey and Tiger was tuckered too, so it didn't take long before he was ready to join Dolly on the mattress they had laid on the earth outside the house. It was evening and the mosquitos were out in force. Dolly and Tiger were swotting themselves constantly. I remembered that I had a spare mosquito net, so I got it out of the truck and tied it up to some branches around their bed. Tiger thanked me profusely, and the last thing I saw before I bade them all goodnight was Tiger gathering all five dogs to sleep with both he and Dolly upon the bed.

I would have loved to have returned and heard the stories those two friends had to tell, but I had an urgent appointment in Darwin so I high-tailed it out of there, and by the time I returned to the Old Man's house, Tiger, Dolly and the five dogs were gone. Old Man was on the verandah with his three dogs lying beside his bed. I said I was sorry to have missed the old fella.

'No worries,' said Old Man, 'Tiger, he might come to that party. Big party happening next week. Lot of people coming. You coming too, alright?'

'Yes, sure Old Man, I'll be there.'

It was going to be a big event. Old Man had decided to have his wake before he died! He wanted to hear all the nice things people had to say about him, now.

\*\*\*

On the edge of the floodplain near the track to Cannon Hill, with the summit of Ubirr in the distance, the Rangers had brought in sand for a stomping ground. They bordered it with Macassan flags that waved gaily in the breeze, and had erected marquees under which so many old friends sat in the shade and chatted with Old Man as he was wheeled among them. Politicians and well-wishers made their speeches in thanks for all that he had done in his long lifetime, while smoke rose from nearby piles of earth under which cooked dugong and wild pig. Painted tribesmen, who had come from afar, danced on the sand as Old Man watched with his glasses tied to the back of his head, nodding in appreciation. I was glad to be there, and honoured when he asked me to wheel him over to the fire-pit to check whether the dugong was ready. But in my heart a sad fact dampened my spirits. This felt like a goodbye, a last chance for Old Man to say farewell to all these friends.

The time was drawing near when he would be gone from here.

\*\*\*

I felt that any story of Old Man's should have his signature upon it, but rather than a written signature, it should be more personal: a footprint, for instance. Aboriginal folk can tell just from looking at a footprint who it belongs to.

I asked Old Man what he thought about this idea and whether we could make a print of his foot.

'He alright, no matter,' he said, 'where you want to make him?'

'Out in the garden, Old Man, there's some good earth there.'

I held his foot down firmly, and we examined the print.

'Good one,' said Old Man approvingly.

It seemed appropriate that Old Man's signature was made of the earth to which he would soon return. There was no more to be said.

I thanked Old Man, and wheeled him back inside.

\*\*\*

Old Man's footprint.

## OLD MAN'S STORY

Months had passed and the Old Man was looking so very thin now, he had lost a lot of weight, and I was really anxious one morning when he asked me to move him out of the house and up to Cannon Hill.

'My country singing out for me,' was all that he said, his chin shaking.

It didn't take long to load his few possessions into the truck: mattress and blankets, mozzie net, a few clothes, glasses, pipe and his wheelchair. He was watching the television while I loaded the truck, and on the screen US President George Bush was telling the people of the world that they were either with America, or, for sure, against. Old Man sat, hunched silently in front of the screen, shaking his head. He said nothing as I helped him into the truck, but as we drove out of there he suddenly struck the dashboard with his hand, and exclaimed loudly, 'ONE WORLD!'

To which I could only reply, 'Yes, Old Man. One day soon, I hope.'

I realised that this journey would probably be the very last that we would have together, Old Man and me. I stole a glance to my left to imprint on my memory the image of his figure sitting beside me in the truck; just to remind me, always, of these times that we had shared together.

We drove in silence up to the small community of Cannon Hill where some of the houses had recently been renovated. The family that lived there came out of their doors to help me unload Old Man's gear and take it inside, while I made up his bed in one of the rooms and wheeled him up the ramp and into the house when it was ready.

Out of the window reared the massive silhouette of Cannon Hill, and beyond, unseen, the silent presence of Injuwanyjuwa and the nearby cave where he would rest, one day soon. I left shortly after but I took the long way back, past Chicken Hawk where we had taken his portrait before. I stopped beside the water, the breeze moaning softly through the nodding heads of the waterlilies.

It wasn't hard to believe that his country was singing out for him.

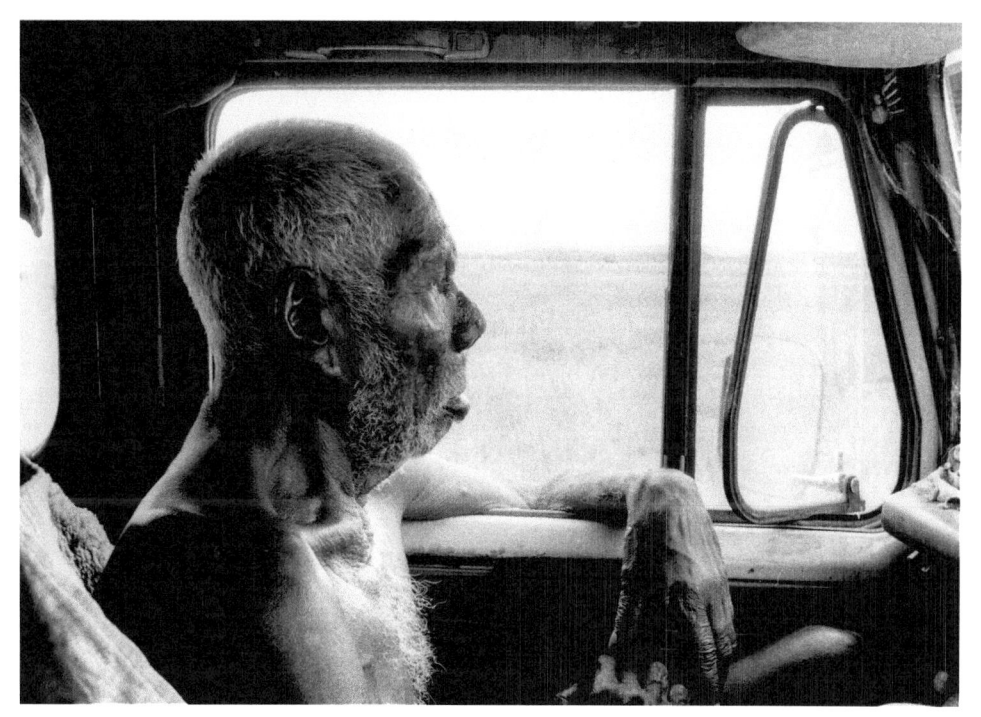

Old Man in the truck.

OLD MAN'S STORY

# LAST DAYS

It was November. The Wet Season was on its way and the night rains were frequent, thundering down upon the tarpaulin, the winds tugging at the canvas. I knew that my time here at East Alligator River was limited. The Rangers were looking to close the campground shortly and I would have to move on.

I would miss the campsite and the characters that lived there: the timid little dove that crept among the leaves beside my table each morning; the family of crows that lived in the ironwood tree above me; the evening calls of the black cockatoos; and the honk of the magpie geese as they flew overhead in the night.

After such a promising start, however, the Wet Season came to a grinding halt. The skies cleared and the rains kept away for a while, so I took the muddy track up to Cannon Hill to see how Old Man was going, and he was going very well. He had moved and was now installed in his old house from the days when he used to live there, and Christine, one of the Aboriginal Rangers' mothers, was looking after him. She was making sure that he took his medicine, and was also taking some trouble to cook him the food that he liked, for she reckoned that he looked far too skinny and needed feeding up. She was hosing out the verandah, clearing away the cobwebs when I arrived, and as we talked Old Man awoke from an afternoon nap and, looking a little blinky, said hello. He looked really well. Christine had cut his hair really short and trimmed his beard, and he was wearing a clean white singlet and shorts. He looked downright dangerous. He pinched one of Christine's cigarettes, and she scolded him for smoking.

I looked around and noticed that the pipe was gone.

'She alright, but yabber yabber too much,' he said, with a mischievous glint in his eye.

I said I was off to Darwin for some provisions. Before I left the house, Christine gave me a shopping list as long as your leg.

'Food for the Wet,' she said, as pressed it into my hand with some money.

'Hmm, looks like it might be a long one too,' I said, as I put it in my pocket.

Days later I took the shopping back up to Cannon Hill and Old Man and I sat out on the verandah in the setting sun.

'I have to leave soon, Old Man, now this job is finished,' I said sadly.

'When you goin?' he asked.

'End of the month, Old Man, before the rain floods me in,' I replied.

'Right,' he said, quietly.

'Going to be hard to leave here, Old Man,' I said, after a pause.

He nodded.

It was going to be a beautiful evening and a full moon would be rising over Cannon Hill, so I wheeled him outside to a clear spot in front of the house, built a small fire for him and pulled up a chair alongside. The day darkened and the full moon rose slowly into the purple sky. It would be our last moon.

We sat there, quietly together. It was a moment of perfect peace that I will never forget. Just Old Man and me, sitting beside the fire by the light of the moon.

So, finally, it was time for me to say my goodbyes and get going before the Wet Season began in earnest, for the storms were coming in thick and fast. I needed one last picture to finish Old Man's book for him, so I walked up to Ubirr where the rock pools were now filled with rainwater, teeming with tadpoles. One pool was special to me, for in its midst was a heart-shaped rock.

After all the time that we had spent together, Old Man and me, it seemed appropriate that I should sign off with an image that symbolized the love that I felt for him, and for his country too. But in its simple shape and meaning, it stood for the one thing that matters to us all.

I made my entry in the Ranger's daily journal before I left for the very last time:

*Thankyou to the old people who shared their story with us.*
*Love is the only way.*
*One world.*

I made one final trip into Darwin to buy a last present for Old Man.

The fateful day came, and I knew that I would have to go and say goodbye to him, for the monsoon rains had come, and East Alligator was about to be cut off by rising floodwaters. I had bought some chocolate biscuits and tobacco, and with the taste of ashes in my mouth, drove up to the house.

He was sitting on his bed, wide awake.

I opened the chocolate biscuits, and we munched on them as we talked about the good times that we had had together. I opened the pack of tobacco and rolled cigarettes for both of us. As the smoke rose to the ceiling I told him that his book was safe and that he need not worry. He nodded and pointed at the packet of biscuits. As I unwrapped one for him and one for me, I gave him my present from Darwin.

His third, and last, Peterson pipe.

## OLD MAN'S STORY

He was delighted.

Only then was it time for me to leave.

I took a deep breath, and I sensed he knew what I was going to say.

'I got to go, Old Man.'

'Yeah right, true.'

Then his skinny arms were around me. We gave each other a long embrace, a growling groan in his throat as he held me there.

'You done good job, Old Man,' I said, as I patted his back, 'your father, when he see you, he will say, you done hardest job.'

He nodded.

Heart-shaped rock, Ubirr.

I rose to go. We clasped each other's hands and looked each other in the eye.
'Boh boh, Old Man,' I whispered.
'Boh boh, my friend,' I heard him say.

*** 

Old Man passed away, six months later, on the 23rd May.
Every time I hear a crow calling, I feel him saying, 'Hey! Where's my story?'
So, Old Man, here it is.

# AFTERWORD

The recording of *Old Man's Story* took several months, comprising nine hours of tape in all, made in several sessions — some lengthy, some not — dictated very much by Old Man's state of health. His emphysema could leave him weak and breathless so I just made sure I was available when he felt like putting some words down. When he did, we would make for some choice spot in his country where he could sit down and gather his thoughts before giving me the nod. Once he was done, I had to play back the tapes and transcribe word for word what he had said onto a computer, and when that was complete I would read the printed hardcopy back to him to ensure that there were no mistakes.

In writing down his story I followed the example as set by Stephen Davis when he transcribed Old Man's words for *Kakadu Man*, Bill Neidjie's first book, in which the words appear in a versal format rather than linear. Old Man used to speak slowly, and paused frequently, and so by following the versal format we gain an impression of his voice. It also allows some 'air' to appear within his words, allowing us to fully absorb what he has just said.

As the recordings were made over several months I found that he had repeated himself somewhat on several occasions, so in the process of editing the final version I discarded some of the repetition. I also moved a few sections around so that there was a better flow to the story, but apart from that, the words that you read are basically what Old Man said.

Each time I read them, all I hear is his voice.